The Loan Officer's Complete Guide To

MARKETING & SELLING MORTGAGE SERVICES

Mortgage Bankers Association of America
The National Association of Real Estate Finance

David L. Hershman

Library of Congress Cataloging-in-Publication Data

Hershman, David L.
    The loan officer's complete guide to marketing & selling mortgage services / David L. Hershman ; edited by Robert Linthicum.
        p.   cm.
    Includes bibliographical references and index.
    ISBN 1-55738-141-0
    1. Mortgage loans—Marketing.   I. Linthicum, Robert. II. Title.
III. Title: Marketing & selling mortgage services.
HG2040.15.H47   1991
332.7′2′0688—dc20   90-19679
                                                                 CIP

Printed in the United States of America

BB

    2   3   4   5   6   7   8   9   0

Table of Contents

Preface

Selling is neither a book, rate sheet or flyer, nor is it goals, objections or speeches. Selling is passion.

Successful salespeople are emotional, high-performance people with the ability to persuade. But persuasive technique is not an end in itself. Top originators understand the importance of service, responsiveness, integrity, dependability, and professionalism in meeting their personal and professional goals.

In this book, successful players from throughout the mortgage lending industry divulge practical, usable sales and marketing techniques. This organized bundle of tools is intended to help originators more fully understand their jobs, market themselves, manage their time, service their customers, and reach their sales potential. The techniques described in this book are easily transferable to other sales fields in the financial services industry.

Acknowledgements

This book would not have been possible without the significant contributions of the sales trainers of mortgage banking. There were also important works contributed by several members of the industry. The following is a list of people whose work made this book what it is today.

Contributors	*Company*
Jack Davis	Jack Davis and Associates
William H. Evans	Institute of Professional Training
James C. Pratt	Pratt/Duncan Group
James L. Hennessy, Jr.	Security Pacific Financial Services, Inc.
Roko Paskov, Ph.D.	Speaker & Consultant
Gaye Greene	Sibley Mortgage Corporation
Anthony Mills	American Residential Mortgage Corporation
Thomas Morgan	American Residential Mortgage Corporation
John Terveer	Superior Service Mortgage
Bradley S. Chapman	Syracuse Securities, Inc.
Walter H. Rissmeyer	Jersey Shore Savings and Loan Association
Mary White	AmeriStar Financial Corporation

Bob Tarrant	South States Mortgage Corporation
Gerald Stewart	Equitable Mortgage Company
Laura Lane Siegal	The Leader Mortgage Company
Timothy Sepherd	Fireman's Fund Mortgage Corporation
Larry Richling	First Mortgage Trust
Richard A. Gillespie	GMAC Mortgage Corporation
Curt Culver	MGIC
Daniel Gilbert	Rock Financial Corporation

I would like also to thank the MBA for their support of this project and those around me who have endured project after project—especially Sean, Michelle and Brenda.

1

The Originator's Functions and Responsibilities

"An originator's function is to originate, or sell, mortgages."

It's true—the originator's primary goal is to find and develop customers who need funds. But an originator's function is subject to interpretation. Consider the following questions regarding the originator's role:

- Is it the company's responsibility to market to the target market (Realtors, builders, and/or the general public), or is it the originator's?

- When a credit report arrives at the office indicating an applicant is prone to slow payments, is it the processor's or originator's responsibility to contact the applicant?

- Is the originator to sell products that are best for the applicant or products that bring the company the most profit?

- Is it the underwriter's job to determine that further documentation is necessary for final approval, or the originator's job to get complete documentation up front?

1

- If a note is incorrectly executed at settlement, whose job is it to get the applicant to re-execute—the settlement department's or the originator's?

- To what level of service must an originator perform?

In a written survey of active Realtors, the Mortgage Bankers Association of America found that a Realtor recommends an average of three lenders to a potential homebuyer. Homebuyers usually follow such recommendations. Therefore, personal and professional relationships with local Realtors are your best and most consistent sources of business.

Realtors are most interested in working with lenders who take the time to develop this relationship, and who follow up after the sale. You must become that lender. You must track the status of every loan package, and be sure the customer is satisfied. Why? Because high quality service wins *repeat business*—your professional lifeblood.

Some important points about your role as an originator:

- The majority of originators represent their company's "front line" in sales. Your primary target? The Realtor.

- Mortgage companies vary widely in their level of originator support. Most companies do not back their originators with organized sales or marketing efforts. Some *give* originators business, for example, builder-owned mortgage companies.

- Once business is in the door, the key to service is a good loan application. Why?
  —A complete loan application enables the processor to submit quickly.
  —Chasing required documents after-the-fact wastes time you should be spending selling.
  —Underwriting the file at loan application decreases the chance of last minute, unexpected bad news and gives you time to correct problems.
  —Support staff will recognize your top-quality service standards. A complete loan application garners their

much-needed support. A team effort helps you reach your goals.

The following exhibits outline a system for taking consistent, complete, and professional applications.

Exhibit 1-1:   How to Take a Great Loan Application

Follow this logic chain to see why a great loan application is essential:

> The key to making money in mortgage banking is repeat business.
>
> The key to repeat business is moving loans quickly.
>
> The key to moving loans quickly is doing the job up front.
>
> The key to doing the job up front is taking a complete loan application.
>
> Good service means repeat business and staying out of the back room. Remember—your business is in the field.

The fundamentals of taking a great loan application:

> Talk to clients *directly*, reviewing the list of items necessary to complete the application. Convey to them that you want to give them great service, and to give them great service they must provide these items. Assure them that you are a financial expert and these are the tools of your trade.
>
> You should be able to obtain 98 percent of any required written explanations at application time using the following guidelines:
>
> - Ask for exact employment dates and income history.
> - Ask about credit history; pinpoint any problems. Look for indicators of bad credit.
> - Order an instant credit report.
>
> Have a complete "extra forms file" that includes disclosures and a real estate schedule.
>
> Partially fill in the loan application from the contract and the purchaser information sheet.
>
> Leave no blank spaces; provide totals where necessary.
>
> Assemble the loan file the same day, preferably immediately after application.
>
> Indicate whether the liquid assets figure includes deposit funds or if the figure is exclusive of deposit funds.
>
> Obtain current credit balances.

Exhibit 1-1   (Continued)

Be specific when asking for additional items. For example, when requesting a lease, ask if the lease is current, expired, or month-to-month.

Read *everything* you collect, as you collect it. Underwrite as you take the application.

Read product guidelines before taking the application.

Reveal qualification problems or other obstacles only after consulting the Realtor.

Use black ink. Certain shades of blue photocopy poorly.

Take the loan application in the Realtor's office—the exposure is a marketing tool in itself.

Exhibit 1-2:   Information Required to Complete a Loan Application

---

Items the Realtor provides:

Copy of the ratified contract, and any ratified addenda thereto.

Copy of the listing card.

Copy of the earnest money deposit check (which should be a certified check or cashier's check).

Information about the purchaser(s):

Full names of all purchasers as they will appear on the title.

Social security numbers of all purchasers. (For FHA loans, regulations require both social security numbers and picture identification.)

Present addresses of all purchasers.

For purchasers residing in their present homes for less than two years, a two-year address history.

Purchaser's home and office phone numbers.

Required employment information:

The applicant's employer's name and address. The applicant must also identify a contact person to whom you can send an employment verification form.

- An explanation for any gaps in the two-year employment history.
- For transferees, a relocation letter detailing date of transfer, salary, change of location, and any relocation benefits.

If the applicant has been in his or her current job for less than two years, the previous employer's name and address. Again, the applicant must identify a contact person for verification purposes.

Confirmation of the applicant's salary via a year-to-date pay stub and W-2s for the last two years. (VA requires retention of an original pay stub.)

Exhibit 1-2 (Continued)

If any variable income (such as commissions, part-time income, bonuses, overtime, or interest income) is being used to qualify the applicant, two years' signed federal tax returns, and W-2s and/or 1099s.

If the applicant is self-employed, two years' signed federal individual returns, and corporate returns, if any. Also, a year-to-date profit and loss and balance sheet.

If the applicant has been a student during the past two years, a diploma or transcript.

Other income information:

Rental income. Copy of a current lease of at least one year in length.

Alimony and child support. If used for qualification, a copy of the divorce decree and ratified terms of property settlement. Request proof of payment at application.

Income from notes held. Copy of the ratified note and tax returns if interest was reportable during the previous calendar year.

Retirement, social security, and disability income. Copy of the award letter and the latest check. Copy of an end-of-the-year statement, if applicable. Social Security income will appear on the applicant's tax returns.

Assets:

Bank accounts. Names of banks, addresses, account numbers, types of accounts and current balances. Use average balances for checking accounts. For all accounts, copies of the three most recent statements.

Stocks and bonds. Copies of certificates or of recent (within 30 days) broker statements with holdings listed. For mutual funds, copies of recent statements.

Life insurance. Cash value, but only if being used for down payment.

Vehicles. Year, make, and value. Copy of the title if the vehicle is under four years old and with no outstanding lien.

Exhibit 1-2   (Continued)

Real estate. Address and market value. If free and clear, the deed of release, deed, or proof of mortgage payoff.

Present home. Copy of sales contract, settlement sheet, and/or lease.

Gift letter. Donor capacity must be verified via a form the financial representative will provide. Funds must appear in an account.

Liabilities:

Credit cards. Account numbers, outstanding balances, and recent statements.

Loans. Auto, mortgage, personal, and student. Names of institutions, addresses, account numbers, outstanding balances, monthly payments, and terms remaining. Copies of payment coupons or statements.

Alimony and child support. Copy of ratified decree and property settlement.

VA loans:

Certificate of eligibility. Form DD-214 (Separation of Service) is required to obtain certificate of eligibility. If the applicant is on active duty, a statement of service signed by the Commanding Officer or Personnel Officer. (The certificate must be updated before application.) If active duty, Form DD-1747 (authorization to live off base) from the housing office. Transfer orders, if applicable.

Payments to be made at application:

Application fee. Include the cost of appraisal and the credit report.

One half of one percent of the loan amount for refinances. To be credited at settlement.

Present home:
    Listing
    Sales contract
    Settlement sheet (if sold within the last year)
    Name and address of landlord
    Deed and deed of trust (for refinances only)

Exhibit 1-3: Peer Review of Mortgage Loan Applications— The "Buddy System"

These guidelines detail a review system for new applications, to improve the quality of originations and minimize future problems.

Policy:

> Every new loan application the originator takes shall be reviewed by another originator within twenty-four hours of submission.

Process:

> Timing. The originator submits the application to his or her buddy by 5:00 pm the day following application. Each buddy shall accomplish this review by 5:00 pm the day after he or she receives the application from the originator.

> Buddy selection. The Branch Manager pairs buddies, taking care to match experienced with new originators. Buddies may be changed as warranted.

> Trainee originators. Originators in training shall buddy review all loan applications during their specified training period. The Branch Manager shall review reports and loans that trainees originate.

> Alternate buddy. If a buddy is unavailable during the required twenty-four hour period, the originating representative is responsible for securing an alternate buddy, usually the Branch Manager.

> Report. The buddy report will include a review of the following:

> - Program description and rate lock. Is it correct?
> - Private mortgage insurance/mortgage insurance premium coverage. Was it disclosed correctly, if necessary?
> - Completeness of application. Did the originator request missing items?
> - Qualification. Does the applicant qualify? Was qualification done correctly? Did the originator overlook any issues which may effect qualification calculations?
> - File set-up. Is set-up complete and orderly?
> - Additional documentation. Are there additional items needed?

Exhibit 1-3   (Continued)

- Additional forms. Are there additional forms needed?
- Good faith. Was the good faith estimate disclosure adequate?
- Timeliness. Did the originator submit the file to his or her buddy within the allotted twenty-four hour period?
- File returned to originator: If the file is inadequate or incomplete for processing or approval under the program, the reviewing party shall return it to the originating representative.

Action on report. After the originator cures any problems, the buddy returns the report to him or her for sign-off and forwarding to the Branch Manager.

Distribution of report. All reports shall be distributed to the Branch Manager, who will review them, place a copy of each report in the processor's file, and return the original to the originating representative.

The objective of the buddy system is to produce high-quality applications and to prevent emergencies at every stage of the lending process. This system allows new originators to learn by reviewing applications before taking on their own originations. Further, when experienced originators are paired with trainees, the experienced originator gains management and underwriting skills.

All originators must support the buddy review system for it to function effectively, without an increase in processing time. Application review can't be performed by one person, and originators must understand that this important quality control technique makes their jobs easier.

Exhibit 1-4:   Timing and Contents of the Loan Application

These guidelines are designed to help the originator establish and maintain consistent levels of speed and quality in the application process, with fast, accurate processing and a high-quality result.

Recommended Application Policies

Appointments. The originator shall contact the client directly before taking the application, to both arrange an appointment and specify the items required to complete the application. The originator shall take the applications in person, in either the Realtor's or mortgage company's office. (The Realtor's office is best.) Avoid taking applications in the house being purchased.

Content. The originator shall submit a *complete* loan application. Application content is detailed in "Requirements for Documentation."

Set-up. The originator shall set up all applications completely, including all internal documents.

Timing. The originator shall submit complete loan applications to his or her buddy by 5:00 pm the day after application.

Exceptions to timing. The only allowable exception to the above guidelines is in the case of an incomplete loan application. The originator shall submit the application to his or her buddy by 5:00 pm the day following receipt of complete information, along with a memo stating the date of receipt for Truth in Lending conformance.

Buddy review. Each buddy shall accomplish review of applications received by 5:00 pm on the day after receipt of the other originator's applications.

Report to agent. The originator shall summarize loan application results by 5:00 pm the day following application.

Loan Application Packets

The originator shall take the loan application on forms the mortgage company provides, and shall segregate conventional and government loan application packets.

Extra Forms File

The originator shall develop his or her own extra forms file, containing supplies of standard and miscellaneous forms as needed.

Exhibit 1-5: Things to Watch for At Loan Application

New home. The originator must admonish the applicant and agent to advise him or her of any actions that change the sales price of the subject property, and that they must submit such changes as they occur.

Maiden name credit report. If married less than one year, or if credit appears anywhere under the maiden name.

Business credit report. If separate corporation or entity.

New accounts. Have the applicants moved recently? Have they rolled over a certificate of deposit recently? Look at balances and dates of auto loans and other types of loans.

Bad credit. Ask about their credit history.

Job gaps. Ask for exact employment dates and the reason for any periods of unemployment.

Child support.

Account balance increases or gifts. Look for any savings amounts which are unusual for the applicant's occupation. Ask how long the applicant has maintained the balance.

Variable income. Ask if the income figure provided represents salary only and no overtime or bonuses.

Property. Check condominiums and planned unit developments against FHA/VA lists. For conventional condominiums, check conventional lists and presale letter.

Investor loan. What are they doing with present properties?

Equity advance. Ensure that the applicant is going to settlement on the present home first, unless they provide adequate notice and a relocation letter. (The applicant may change his or her mind after application if a relocation offer is low.)

Rental lease. Ask if the current lease is in effect or month-to-month.

Refinance. Are there late payments on the mortgage?

Exhibit 1-6: Summary of Items to Request Concerning Property

Sales contract. If not a refinance, the ratified sales contract and any addenda.

Copy of listing. If not for sale by owner, refinance, or a new home. A refinance will require a copy of the deed, a written explanation for refinance with the use of any funds received and a HUD I for sale or refinance within the past twenty-four months.

Appraisal. The mortgage company orders the appraisal.

Appraisal condition satisfaction. Final inspection by the mortgage company, appraiser, or agency.

Well or septic certification. A settlement condition, must be dated within 45 days of settlement.

Termite certification. A settlement condition which must be dated within 45 days of settlement. Subject property must be free of termites and termite damage, or treated and/or repaired.

Title insurance. A settlement condition an attorney must supply within 90 days of settlement.

Survey. A settlement condition an attorney must supply within 90 days of settlement.

Hazard insurance. The applicant must have dwelling coverage for at least the loan amount, with the correct mortgagee clause, property address, name, and other data, along with a paid receipt for one year of coverage. A full policy is required—binders may be unacceptable. Six months rent loss insurance required for two- to four-family investor loans.

Certificate of insurance. For condominiums, the certification that the mortgage company has been added to the master policy.

Road maintenance agreement. If the subject property is not located on a publicly maintained street.

Special assessments. Fees on property. Condominium documents and proof of approval.

**Exhibit 1-7:   Summary of Items to Request at Loan Application
for Income Verification**

Salary and verification of employment. A year-to-date stub and two
years' W-2s.

Overtime. A year-to-date stub and two years' year-end pay stubs, or
an employer letter detailing base salary, overtime, average hours
worked, and the rate of overtime for the past two years. Two years'
W-2s.

Bonuses. A year-to-date and two years' year-end pay stubs, or an
employer letter detailing base salary, bonuses, and the rate of bonuses for the past two years. Two years' W-2s.

Commission. Two years' signed tax returns, W-2s, or 1099s. A year-
to-date pay stub with expense information. An employer letter detailing base salary, commissions for past two years, and/or two
year-end pay stubs with detailed sources of income.

Self-employment. Two years' signed tax returns and year-to-date
earnings. Ask about ownership interest. Determine if the applicant
owns 25 percent or more of a corporation or partnership. If so, get
two years' corporate or partnership tax returns and a business credit
report.

Interest and dividends. Two years' signed tax returns and year-to-
date broker or bank statements.

Note(s) held. Copy of ratified note(s) and signed tax returns if income was reported last year.

Rental income. Copies of ratified, current, one-year leases. If not
current, tenant letters, tax returns, or previous leases.

Alimony and child support. Copy of a ratified agreement or decree.
Proof of stable payments—tax forms (for alimony), court records,
cancelled checks, or deposit records (for child support) for the past
year.

Social Security. Tax forms, 1099s, award letters, change of status letters, or copies of checks or check stubs with the original award letter.

Employee benefits. Letter from employer itemizing any employee
benefits.

Exhibit 1-7   (Continued)

Future raises. Letter from employer stating certainty, time, and amount of raise.

Explanations required.
    Job gap one month or more.
    Any decrease in income.
    Complex job history.
    Many job changes.

Exhibit 1-8:   Summary of Items to Request at Loan Application for Verification of Funds

Bank account. Three months' bank statements. Order Verification of Deposit (VOD).

Stocks and bonds. Three months' statements. Order VOD, copy of certificate, or proof of liquidation.

Quasi-liquid accounts. Three months' statements. Order VOD or proof of liquidation for certificates of deposit, individual retirement accounts, or pension plans.

Deposits. Copies of bank checks, or a copy of the front and back of cancelled personal deposit checks.

Gift. Gift letter, donor verification (such as a bank statement), and proof of receipt of funds. If an FHA loan, order a new VOD.

Sale of asset. Bill of sale and proof of receipt of funds. Sales contract and settlement sheet upon sale of the applicant's present home. A relocation letter for an equity advance.

Borrowing. Approval and terms of loan and receipt of funds.

Second trust. If commercial, approval and terms.

Seller concessions. Must be included in contract and verified on HUD I after closing.

Company reimbursement. Relocation letter detailing benefits. Proof of receipt if required for transaction.

Miscellaneous. Copy of note held, copy of will or letter from executor, copy of retirement statement, verification of receipt of funds for all of the above.

Explanations. Recent accounts or increases in account balances.

Exhibit 1-9:   Summary of Items to Request at Loan Application to Verify Credit

Mortgages. Verification of mortgage. Copy of most recent statement and/or end-of-year statement. If a twelve-month payment history is not reported on statement or credit report, twelve months' cancelled checks. If the mortgage can't be verified, or if it's foreign or private, secure tax forms, cancelled checks, and a copy of the note.

Loans. Verification of credit if history not on credit report. Copy of the most recent statement.

Credit cards. Credit report. One for each applicant or married couple. Maiden name report if married within past year. Corporate report if the applicant owns 25 percent or more of corporation or partnership, and income being used to qualify is derived from the same. Copy of statement if balance and/or payment is refused.

Quasi-credit. Rental verification, child-care statement, property settlement, separation agreement, or divorce decree. Utilities checks or letters from utility companies.

Proof of payoff. For all loans to be paid off or any past due accounts that must be brought current.

Free and clear. Car title. Deed of release or mortgage payoff. If not available, then tax returns showing no interest deduction and other monthly obligations such as taxes, insurance and HDA fees.

Explanations. Written explanations for any late payment, regardless of significance. More significant problems require additional documentation—court documents and attorney letters. Applicants must explain recent inquiries.

Exhibit 1-10: Contract Addenda to Request at Loan Application

The originator must request a ratified copy of the contract and all addenda thereto. Often, the originator may request corrections via an addendum for:

The removal of any contingencies contained in the contract. For example, contingent upon the sale of another house, or upon home inspection. The only exception to this is a standard housing inspection contingency which automatically expires if no notification is made. Any contingency requires an addendum removing it.

Change in the loan amount from contract loan amount. A change upward or a significant change downward may require an addendum. Any change may affect the seller, e.g., the cost of discount points. An exception is when the mortgage company rounds down to the nearest $50, or the mortgage insurance premium is added to the loan amount (if the contract specifies that mortgage insurance premium is to be financed).

Adding mortgage insurance premium or funding fee to be financed, if a higher loan amount is not specified. This also affects the seller's cost of discount points.

Changing the address or legal description of the subject property. Any mistake in the contract, whether discovered by the listing, appraisal, or the survey, must be corrected with an addendum.

Correct purchasers. The addition or subtraction of co-borrowers, even if required by the mortgage company, must be shown by an addendum. Wrong names or spelling must also be corrected.

FHA amendatory clause. Any difference in the sales price requires an addendum.

New homes. Any options added after application will change the sales price. Though an addendum will be completed, often it's not sent to the mortgage company or comes after the appraisal is finished, which will now be too low. Make sure future addenda are requested at loan application.

Exhibit 1-10 (Continued)

Removing financial concessions. Seller cash concessions may *not* be allowed under the financing program specified in the contract. An addendum may be necessary to remove such concessions, or change the purpose of concessions. For example, "Will credit $4,000 towards repairs" may be changed to, "Will credit $4,000 towards closing costs but not prepaids."

Seller certification. Certification that the contract constitutes the entire agreement. (Required for FHA.)

Exhibit 1-11: Explanations to Obtain At Loan Application

The following is a list of handwritten explanations the applicant must give the originator at loan application. Remember, an explanation is always easier to get at the application table than on the phone later.

Job gap. Always ask exact dates of employment. Any gap of one month or more requires an explanation. Gaps are acceptable if there is only one job (for example, with leaves of absence) or going from part-time to full-time status. Always check the pay stubs and W-2s at application to ensure that they agree with the applicant's given history.

Complicated job history. A work record with several jobs held concurrently or during the two-year history may require an explanation to prevent the history from appearing unstable. Self-employment with changes in corporate status is another example of a complicated history that would require an explanation.

New accounts. Ask the applicant if he or she has opened any accounts within the last six months. The applicant must explain new loans and deposit accounts. While an obvious situation would involve a recent transferee, an explanation is still required. If the applicant has a certificate of deposit, ask if they recently rolled it over. These funds may show up as a new account. The applicant may have taken out new loans to pay the earnest money deposit. This may be allowed if explained and paid off before settlement. VA may allow this in any event.

Increase in account. Inquire if the balances of any accounts of more than a few thousand dollars have been stable for the past few months. Any substantial increase must be explained. Many times, applicants "shuffle" money directly before purchasing a house. You may discover an unreported new loan taken out to cover the down payment or simply a misplaced digit, the discovery of which could present problems before settlement. Read the bank statements.

Late payments. Take care to ask the applicants at the table if they've ever had credit problems. Give them the opportunity to divulge this information when they say, "I tore up my credit cards" or, "I have had some trouble with that organization." Any late payment, even resulting from a once-in-a-lifetime vacation, requires an explanation.

Exhibit 1-11   (Continued)

Judgments, bankruptcies, and tax liens. These more serious credit problems require a more detailed explanation and backup documentation.

Refinance. The reason for refinance, no matter how obvious, must be given in writing at loan application, including the use for any cash out.

Decrease in salary. The reason for any job change or other occurrence resulting in a significant decrease in salary.

Exhibit 1-12: Loan Application—Self-employed

The self-employed borrower is one who actually works for him or herself—i.e., borrowers not employed by a corporation, or controlling a substantial part of their employing entity. Usually, 25 percent ownership in
the employing entity will result in the determination that the borrower is
self-employed, although a stricter standard is sometimes used.

Types of Self-employed Applicants

No legal entity involved. The most simple self-employed applicant
is one who is not employed by a separate corporation or other entity, but files with the Internal Revenue Service using a Schedule C
return.

Separate legal entity involved. The borrower may be employed by,
or derive income from, the following:

- Subchapter S corporation.
- Corporation.
- Partnership.
- Other types of joint ventures.
- Farm.

Information an originator must request of an applicant at application:

Two years' individual tax returns and W-2s, or 1099s if on salary
from a corporation or partnership.

Two years' corporate or partnership returns if there is a separate
corporation or partnership.

If the corporate and/or individual returns produce a gap of financial history from the ending date of the return to the time of approval of more than one quarter, the applicant must submit a year-
to-date business profit and loss statement, prepared and signed by a
Certified Public Accountant, and a balance sheet. Also, if the applicant is on salary, the profit and loss statement should include an
income statement detailing the expense amount that represents the

---

Exhibit 1-12: (Continued)

---

applicant's salary. If the applicant's business is a small operation with no accountant, an applicant-prepared profit and loss statement will suffice, but only if accompanied by a signed perjury statement.

Any allowances for income through salary must be supported with further documentation, such as pay stubs.

If a corporation or partnership exists, a business credit report may be required. A report is unnecessary in the case of a Schedule C, because there is no separate legal entity to own assets or incur liabilities.

Exhibit 1-13: Items to Request on Relocations

Copy of transfer orders, if employed by the Federal Government or military. These orders will provide the following information:

Previous location.

Permanent duty station location.

Effective date of transfer.

Any change in salary.

Relocation letter, if employed by a private company. The relocation letter will provide the date and place of relocation, and will detail the following applicant benefits that are usable for qualification:

Closing costs. Is the firm paying some or all of the costs of home purchase and financing? If so, which costs will the firm pay, including the number of points, and for what purposes may points be used? For discount or origination?

Mortgage interest differential. Will the firm pay a periodic supplement to your new mortgage payment? The applicant must detail any supplement precisely, including amount and duration, which must be of three to five years to qualify as income.

Raises. Is the applicant's salary to be adjusted at the new location? If they are to receive a raise, what is the new salary and effective date?

If the applicant is selling a home at his or her previous location, the originator must obtain a ratified settlement sheet (HUD I) detailing proceeds upon sale. If there is any chance that the applicant won't go to settlement on his or her old home before purchasing in the new location, the relocation letter must also detail the following:

Payment of the costs of selling the previous home.

Guaranteed sale of present home and minimum offer price.

Duplicative mortgage payments. The applicant's employing firm must assume responsibility for mortgage payments on the previous dwelling for as long as there exist both current and past mortgages.

Equity advance. How much equity will the applicant's employing firm advance for the present home? Repayment must not be a requirement. An equity advance is not a loan.

Exhibit 1-13   (Continued)

The applicant must provide proof of receipt of the equity advance and/or payment of closing costs if the funds are required to complete the purchase.

If the company's products are unappealing to the target market, there will exist a conflict of interest between the company's expectation of high sales volume and any salesperson's need for *repeat business*. Eventually, something must give.

To become a successful originator, you must understand the scope and boundaries of your functions before you implement objectives, plans, and actions. Your expectations and the company's must correspond. The following is a list of areas in which you and your company need to reach an understanding on your function:

Availability. During what hours and in which geographical limits are you to be available? Similar to the real estate industry, the mortgage business operates at night and on weekends. Your hours must conform to the time that Realtors conduct business.

Originators are usually assigned a specific territory. However, the office may receive calls from all over the United States. Where does your company transact business, and what delineates its market area? What is your territory? Finally, how far will you physically go to service that market area?

Loan application. What comprises a fully documented loan application, executed in accordance with company policy? Who must pursue missing documentation? The originator, or processing staff?

Underwriting. Who is responsible for verifying that applications meet minimum program guidelines? Are the files to be reviewed after the origination process, or is the first review to be submission to the underwriter?

Processing. What follow-up must you conduct while the loan is being processed? Are you to meet with the processor for "status sessions?"

Marketing. Which marketing efforts are the originator's responsibility, and which are the company's? Who is to pay for business cards, originator-focused newspaper advertisements, catering Realtor events, and business lunches? What flyers, rate sheets, and mailings must the company develop in your support?

Settlement. Who is to arrange a settlement date with the closing agent and company? Who reviews standard closing conditions and required documentation with the closing agent?

While the originator's job is to sell loans, every salesperson has an interest in the completion of the transaction, a satisfied customer, and repeat business. A success-oriented originator views support staff as essential team members, and understands the importance of a good working relationship with them. He or she knows "word of mouth" is an invaluable source of new business, and that repeat business and a strong client referral base are key for loan sales success.

The originator's job description is cloudy. Individual circumstances and company practices vary. We've provided some questions to ask yourself and your company to better define your functions. Now let's take a look at the traits and behaviors of successful originators.

The Characteristics of a Successful Originator

"There are two classes of people who tell what is going to happen in the future: Those who don't know and those who don't know they don't know."
— *John Kenneth Galbraith*

If this book could successfully identify top-notch originators before they began their careers, we'd have a popular product. The mortgage industry's originator selection process remains almost trial-and-error, though some scientifically designed tests have emerged. High turnover rates in the mortgage lending industry are testimony to less than precise judgement in selecting and hiring loan originators.

Truth be told, it may be impossible to accurately predict the likelihood of a salesperson's success. But successful originators do have common traits. These are attributes originators should strive to emulate, if they don't already possess them. The following is a list of those qualities, in the areas of work ethic, judgment, intelligence, and attitude.

Work Ethic

Intensity. Originators are much like independent contractors. Once on the street on their own, they are unsupervised, have no time card to punch, and no supervisor looking over their shoulders. It's not unusual for top producers to work sixty to eighty hours per week.

Consistency. To be effective, originators must be consistent. For example, many companies produce newsletters on an irregular, sporadic basis. This is useless for achieving solid name identification. Newsletters are effective only if produced on a consistent basis. The newsletter target market learns what to expect and when to expect it.

Persistence. The key to consistency is persistence. Successful originators rarely take No for an answer. They just keep on coming. A marketing tool or a sales call rarely works on the first or second try—consider the "Rule of 7":

The "Rule of 7" asserts that if you want prospects to buy what you're selling, you must connect with them a minimum of *seven times* within an eighteen month period. Then, and only then, can you reasonably expect prospects to know what you can do for them and induce them to act. These connections with your prospect can only be successful if each communication clearly indicates that you understand his or her problem and have something that can solve it, and that each connection is with the same person.

You might apply this principle on a more condensed scale. For example, make seven "connections" in a three-month period.

Command. Good loan officers are knowledgeable. Great loan officers exercise command over knowledge. Knowledge is knowing the answer; command gives us control over the entire process. Knowledge makes us an originator; command makes us an expert. Successful originators control their environment instead of letting their environment control them.

Good Judgment

Ethics. Long-term success comes only to those who have reputations for staying "above board." Originators' egos and independence foster ample opportunities and pressures to manipulate. How many originators have made a false promise? How many have been pressured to overlook a fact that would adversely affect the approval process? In the long run, unethical originators lose the respect of top agents who expect to work with professionals.

Professional sales approach. Professional originators don't just drop a rate sheet and run. Good originators assess:

- The target group's needs. Is the target in an area with a heavy concentration of FHA loans or non-FHA approved condominium projects?

- Their competition. Who are your competitors, and why are they successful or unsuccessful? What products do they sell? What marketing tools do they use?

- Their understanding of the mortgage process. We've already discussed the importance of underwriting a loan at application. Successful originators learn every phase of the mortgage process, including underwriting. Originators armed with such knowledge save untold hours at application, and avoid wasting time on lost causes.

- Their knowledge of their product line and company strengths. Realtors love originators who can explain loan types and their product line. Answering any question concerning mortgage products is key to providing professional service.

Decision-making Capacity

Successful originators learn first, sell next. But knowledge is only the first step. The mortgage business is a series of problems with solutions. Originators must have above-average decision making abilities to:

- Know which deals to pursue and which to turn away.

- Use product knowledge to solve such qualification problems as self-employment, short cash, termite damage which sellers refuse to rectify, and many others.

- Package an application in a way that prevents qualification problems and produces approvals where competitors would have failed to do so.

- Choose marketing methods that are appropriate for the target market.

- Recognize their limitations and capitalize on the resources available to expand those limitations.

Positive Attitude

A positive attitude is an originator's most important trait. A successful originator doesn't hear No. Every No represents a Maybe. But a positive attitude is more than persistence. It rallies support staff. A positive attitude empowers originators with the ability to control their environment, turning obstacles into stepping stones of success. And in the highly competitive mortgage market, only the strong survive.

- *Professionalism.* The way you dress, return phone calls, treat clients, and lead your profession separates you, a professional, from the lightweights.

- *Personality.* Personality is the intangible of intangibles. We know that the key to sales is cultivating relationships.

- *Ego.* For any salesperson to inspire people to act, he or she must project confidence and a high level of self esteem. A tentative or "beatdog" attitude will do little to rally your customer's confidence in you or your products.

- *Empathy.* The ability to "walk a mile in another man's moccasins." Originators who are able to understand their customer's needs and concerns will win a stubbornly loyal customer base.

What An Originator Must Know Before Originating

The following is an outline of the information gathering process. In a professional sales approach, preparation is the "information step." The originator must prepare himself or herself with knowledge in the following areas:

- Company goals, organization and background.
- Essentials of mortgage finance.
- Product knowledge.
- Mortgage banking functions.
- The market.

Company Goals, Organization and Background

Company objectives will determine whether management will view your results as successful. For example, if company policy is to maximize jumbo loan volume, management will consider your performance substandard if you write small FHA loans, regardless of volume.

Company organization may have much to do with the your marketing strategy and your ultimate success in loan sales. If company structure features decentralized underwriting, you should emphasize the company's responsiveness in your marketing efforts. Familiarity with the organization and its personnel enables you to recognize available resources such as marketing support, media experts, or staff with proficiency in certain types of approvals.

Who and what is the company? How old is it, and is it a subsidiary of another business? Sister companies provide additional target groups. Its financial status, history, size, tradition, and reputation may provide highlight material for marketing efforts.

Essentials of Mortgage Finance

Though this book focuses on the sales, an originator must understand the basics of mortgage finance, such as:

- How to qualify an applicant.

- How to take a complete loan application.

- The basic sources of mortgages (FHA, VA, Fannie Mae, Freddie Mac, and state bond financing programs) and their advantages, disadvantages, and restrictions. You must have a working knowledge of these sources whether or not you actually sell their products. Why? Because you will be selling against them.

- Mortgage types and their parameters: adjustables, buydowns, growing equity mortgages, balloons, and graduated payment mortgages.

Product Knowledge

Once you have mastered the fundamentals, you must learn the product line and what characteristics differentiate one product from another. Specifications such as acceptable loan-to-value ratios, mortgage insurance requirements, underwriting guidelines, and settlement requirements will determine how you will market the products and to whom. Again, the mortgage industry is basically a series of problems and solutions. Which product will solve which purchaser's problem?

Mortgage Banking Functions

A reputation for "getting the job done" will increase your sales volume. To attain this status, you must have the ability to prepare the mortgage for smooth passage throughout the process. A working knowledge of processing, underwriting, and settlement puts you in the position to use such knowledge to deliver outstanding customer service.

For example, knowledge of processing gives you the capacity to prepare a loan in such a way that it will be processed quickly and without problems. Underwriting knowledge helps to avoid dead ends. Easy settlement completes the process.

A familiarity with the secondary market is desirable, even if it's only rudimentary knowledge. To sell, you must know why certain charges are levied and the importance of each. Interest rate spreads often portend a change in the market that will call for originating different mortgage types, as in the case of an "adjustable rate market" or a "fixed rate market."

The Market

To sell, you must know your market. The basic components of a market area analysis are:

- Loan sizes and types typically generated.
- Number of real estate companies and their market shares.
- Other sources of loans in the area: closing agents, insurance companies, and financial planners.
- Market trends: growth patterns, inventory turnover, and population trends.

Further, you must know the competition and why each of them is or isn't successful. What products do they carry and how are they priced? What level of service do they offer? When do they visit offices and what marketing materials do they use? With what agents have they developed relationships and how close are these ties? What are their weaknesses? Processing time? Limited product menu? Financially weak parent company?

The information or preparation state is an aspect of sales that separates professionals from loan pushers. The following exhibit is just one example of the training originators should be exposed to before "hitting the street."

**Exhibit 1-14: Sample Initiation and Training Program
for Loan Originators**

Orientation:

- History and structure of the organization—organizational chart
- Functions of the organization flow chart
- Goals of the organization
    - Secondary market—how the company achieves profits.
    - Branch organizational chart—vertical flexibility.
    - Cross training and team approach—horizontal flexibility.
    - Quality control up front—quality control manual.
    - Promotion from within—goal parity.
- Personnel orientation
    - Personnel forms.
    - Employee handbook—leave, hours, review, overtime, and work standards.
    - Company meetings.
    - Staff meetings.
    - Status sessions.
    - Sales meetings.
    - Operations meetings—processing and/or settlements.
- Orientation-Introductory letter—Personnel
    - Employment letter to individual and corporation.
    - Introductory letter to staff.
    - Employee handbook.
    - Personnel forms.
    - Operations manual.

Exhibit 1-14 (Continued)

- Materials and tools
  - —Long distance accounting code.
  - —Keys to office and/or building.
  - —Long distance travel card.
  - —Desktop calculator.
  - —Portable calculator.
  - —Office and desk supplies.
  - —Briefcase.
  - —Travel calendar.
- Substantive materials—Manuals
  - —Quality control.
  - —Product specifications.
  - —PMI specifications.
  - —Originations.
  - —Processing.
  - —Settlements.
  - —Underwriting.
  - —Administration.
  - —Reference.
  - —General finance.
- Policy memos
  - —Rate and registration.
  - —Processing.
  - —Settlements.
  - —Underwriting.
  - —Personnel and administration.

Exhibit 1-14   (Continued)

- Loan application
  - —Loan application packets.
  - —Extra form files.
- Marketing materials
  - —Previous marketing materials.
  - —Answering machine and/or "hold" feature—home phone.
  - —Pager and/or car phone.
  - —Business cards.
  - —Map and Realtor listing.
  - —Introductory package for Realtors.
  - —Reference letters.
  - —Classroom training—Orientation, substantive programs.
- Government financing
  - —FHA.
  - —VA.
  - —State Bond Issues.
- Conventional financing
  - —Conforming—Freddie Mac and Fannie Mae.
  - —Jumbo programs.
- Qualifying
  - —Ratio.
  - —Residual.
- PMI
  - —Coverages.
  - —Specifications.

Exhibit 1-14 (Continued)

- Buydowns
  - —Permanent.
  - —Temporary.
- ARMs
  - —Characteristics.
  - —Programs and comparison.
  - —Marketing.
- Miscellaneous products
  - —GEMs.
  - —Balloons.
  - —Second trusts.
  - —Biweekly programs.
- Refinancing
- Procedural
- Originator
  - —Work flow.
  - —Specific responsibilities.
  - —Policies and procedures.
- Loan application
  - —Forms.
  - —Documentation: income, funds, credit, property, and contract.
  - —RESPA/TIL.
  - —"Buddying" the loan application.
- Processing—general
  - —Work flow.
  - —Specific responsibilities.
  - —Policies and procedures.

Exhibit 1-14   (Continued)

- Processing
  - —Set-up case.
  - —Review—verifications, credit report, appraisal, contracts.
  - —Miscellaneous documentation.
  - —Follow-up.
  - —Work-ups.
  - —"Buddying" a loan submission.
  - —Conditions.
- Settlements—general
  - —Work flow.
  - —Specific responsibilities.
  - —Policies and procedures.
- Settlements
  - —Documentation requirements—hazard policy, termite, title.
  - —Binder, survey, flood insurance.
  - —Preparing settlement documents.
  - —Warehousing.
  - —Reviewing attorney package and final documentation.
- Underwriting
  - —Work flow.
  - —Specific responsibilities.
  - —Policies and procedures.
  - —Forms.
- Administration
  - —Specific responsibilities—managers.
  - —Specific responsibilities—receptionist/AA.

Exhibit 1-14   (Continued)

Customer Service and Marketing:

- Customer service
  - —Telephone contact.
  - —Face-to-face contact.
- Sales approaches
  - —Philosophies.
  - —Techniques.

Operational Training—Equipment and Services:

- Telephone system, duplication equipment, postage machine, facsimile machine, computer, typewriter
- Couriers, overnight, long distance, appraisers, credit bureaus, pmi companies

Loan Application:

- Workbook
- Buddy cases
- Mock loan application
- Call-ins
- Field
  - —Loan applications.
  - —Realtor calls.
  - —Training sessions.
  - —Sales meetings.

Processing:

- Workbook
- Set-ups

Exhibit 1-14   (Continued)

- Review mail—monitor status sessions
- Buddy submissions

Settlements:

- Settlement conditions—procure conditions
- Accomplish settlement package

Market Research

Outline Territory:

- Offices-routes
- Builders
- Organizations
- Mailing list

Manager Meetings:

- Introductory package
- Needs of office
- Invitation to sales meeting and/or training

First Office Visit:

- Introductory package
- Rate sheet
- Newsletter

2

The Tools and Systems of Sales

Rate Sheets and Flyers

"The originator is a mortgage company's mouthpiece." That's often the excuse given for the lack of organized marketing efforts by mortgage companies. Because Realtors refer 80 percent of applicants, marketing directly to the public isn't as fruitful as marketing directly to that industry.

If the originator is the industry's mouthpiece, the rate sheet is its megaphone. While few resources have been devoted to studying and evaluating the effectiveness of these sales tools, rate sheets and flyers encompass a large portion of a sales budget, and occupy a large portion of marketing time and other resources.

If a typical originator delivers 200 flyers three times per week, this could amount to an expense of $25,000 yearly for a sales staff of 20 originators. The cost of the time used to create, duplicate, and distribute these flyers could easily double or triple the expense.

And what do we often hear about this mainstay of marketing? "Sales is more than delivering rate sheets!" But we continue to deliver them, so let's spend some time discussing what this sales tool represents.

The Rate Sheet's Purpose

Of course, the rate sheet's primary purpose is to inform Realtors of the mortgage company's rates. The flyer also serves to:

- Give the originator a legitimate reason for being in a Realtor's office.

- Establish name identification for the company and originator.

- Introduce a program and program parameters.

- Introduce a service feature, such as quick approval.

- Demonstrate a full product line.

- Delineate program requirements, for example, information needed for approval.

- Carry other news, such as a recent VA maximum rate change.

Production

There are two primary means of rate sheet/flyer production. One method has the mortgage company develop and print in mass quantities for distribution. This method enables the company to ensure quality marketing products. However, it's inflexible and limits the ability to personalize the information. Further, it's difficult to mass-produce rate sheets with rates changing daily or more often. Conversely, flyers introducing programs or services are appropriate for mass production because the information contained in them changes less frequently.

The other method is creating daily rate sheets. This system (or lack of a system) gives you the flexibility to present different rates and programs on a daily or even hourly basis. Unfortunately, the opportunity for controlling quality and creating marketing homogeneity is practically nil.

Fortunately, there exists some middle ground for these two extremes. The company may print rate sheet masters or outlines of a rate sheet format. Originators then fill in each section with their information. The result is a professional, standardized format.

The master can range from merely a bordered page with the company logo to a more specific outline including rate sheet categories and some program parameters, for example, maximum loan amounts and loan-to-values. You can mass-produce rate sheets in eye-catching color by simply loading colored paper into the photocopier. The following exhibits are examples of such rate sheet masters.

Exhibit 2-1

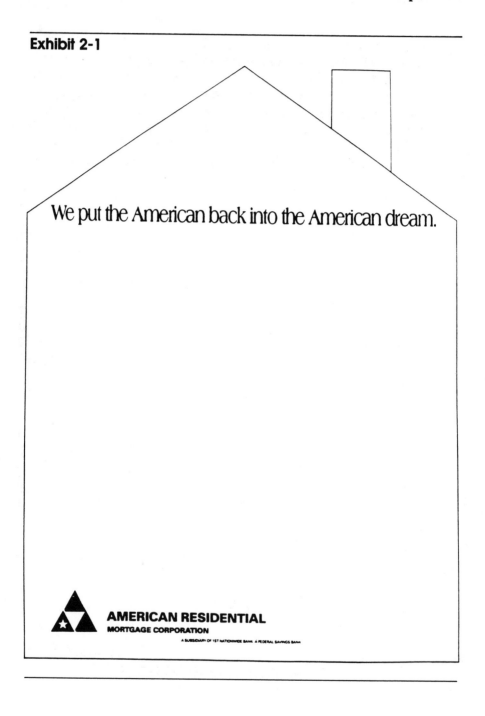

We put the American back into the American dream.

AMERICAN RESIDENTIAL
MORTGAGE CORPORATION
A SUBSIDIARY OF 1ST NATIONWIDE BANK A FEDERAL SAVINGS BANK

Exhibit 2-2

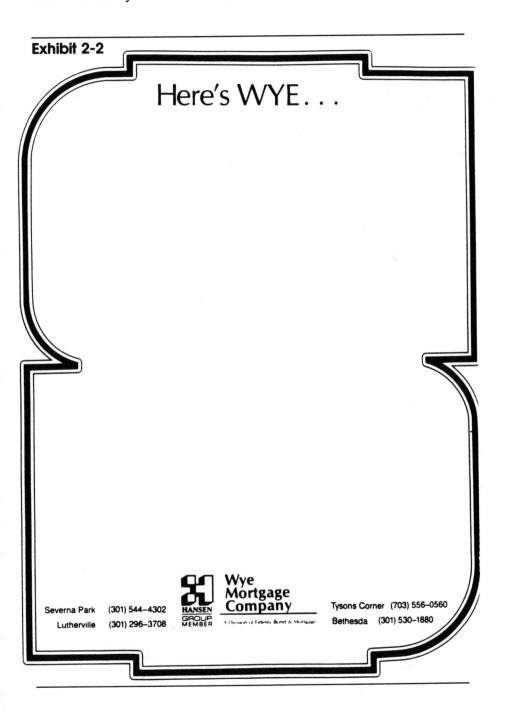

Exhibit 2-3

RATE BULLETIN

Exhibit 2-4

Sibley Mortgage CORPORATION

600 Crossroads Building
2 State Street
Rochester, New York 14614
716-232-1190
1-800-742-5391

24 Hour Priceline
716-232-7275

—— **MORTGAGE MENU** ——

SEE REVERSE FOR EVEN MORE SELECTIONS ⇨

Market Conditions may cause Pricing to change without Notice
This Informational Material is intended to be used by Real Estate Professionals

Branches located in: Albany, Buffalo, Lower Hudson, Rochester, Syracuse, New York • Akron, Ohio / Equal Housing Lender

—— Licensed Mortgage Banker — NYS Banking Department ——

Exhibit 2-5

For some, the only financing option is ARMed and dangerous.

Our 3-2-1 Buydown offers a secure alternative and more buying power.

Your customers are more than likely hearing about the volatility of the Adjustable Rate market. The initial rate on an ARM may look attractive, but there's no guarantee on future rate fluctuation.

Now borrowers can have the benefits of adjustability and the security of a fixed rate product. With **AMERICAN RESIDENTIAL** 3-2-1 buydown we

subsidize the rate. The borrower qualifies at the start rate, which is three percentage points below the note rate. There are two rate adjustment options on this conforming product:

- A 1% increase in payment every six months for a maximum of 18 months.

- A 3/4% increase in payment every six months for a maximum of 24 months.

Home buyers can now plan their future around a secure mortgage payment. No more surprising jumps in monthly expenses, each increase can be anticipated.

AMERICAN RESIDENTIAL is one of the nation's largest mortgage lenders, funding close to $4 billion in home mortgages in 1988. Located in 17 states, with more than 50 offices nationwide, **AMERICAN RESIDENTIAL** is a subsidiary of 1st Nationwide Bank, with $34 billion in assets. A subsidiary of Ford Motor Company, 1st Nationwide is a part of the Ford Financial Services Group.

AMERICAN RESIDENTIAL
MORTGAGE CORPORATION

Please contact me for more information

This information is not an advertisement to extend consumer credit as defined by paragraph 226.24 Regulation Z. It is intended for use by the real estate industry and is not for distribution to the general public.

Exhibit 2-6

LOAN TYPE	TERM	MAXIMUM LOAN/LTV	RATE	

RATES AND DISCOUNT POINTS SUBJECT TO CHANGE DAILY

Exhibit 2-7

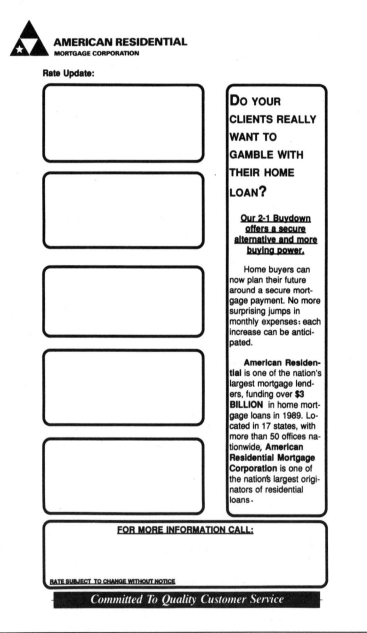

AMERICAN RESIDENTIAL
MORTGAGE CORPORATION

Rate Update:

DO YOUR CLIENTS REALLY WANT TO GAMBLE WITH THEIR HOME LOAN**?**

Our 2-1 Buydown offers a secure alternative and more buying power.

Home buyers can now plan their future around a secure mortgage payment. No more surprising jumps in monthly expenses: each increase can be anticipated.

American Residential is one of the nation's largest mortgage lenders, funding over **$3 BILLION** in home mortgage loans in 1989. Located in 17 states, with more than 50 offices nationwide, **American Residential Mortgage Corporation** is one of the nation's largest originators of residential loans.

FOR MORE INFORMATION CALL:

RATE SUBJECT TO CHANGE WITHOUT NOTICE

Committed To Quality Customer Service

Exhibit 2-8

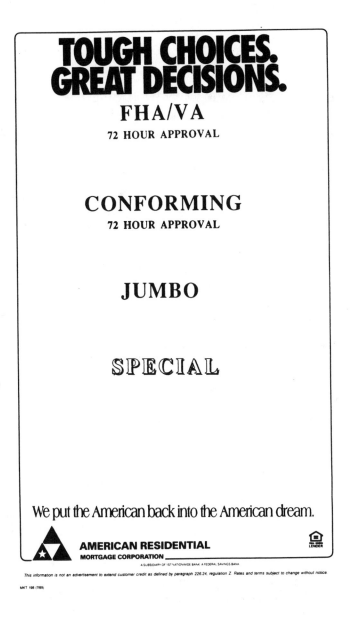

With the advent of personal computers and affordable desktop publishing software, rate sheet production may soon enter a new age.

Composition

There are a few significant issues regarding the composition of rate sheets. How many programs and rates will you present? If yours is a full-service mortgage company, should you list all programs and rate options on the rate sheet, or should you limit the sheet to certain options?

An originator's first reaction is to include every program. You don't know what the Realtor might need that day, and if a program is missing, they might not call. Conversely, too many programs distract the Realtor from the main feature or the program you're featuring. You can't sell everything.

A compromise is to feature three or four programs, listing others available at the bottom of the sheet, for example:

Also available:

No income verification at 80% LTV
Construction loans
Coop loans
Jumbo loans to $2,000,000

Call for details!

Another choice concerns detail. Most Realtors prefer all program parameters on the rate sheet so they don't have to call with questions. But a rate sheet is supposed to make the phone ring from the originator's point of view. So if too much detail prevents them from calling, you've circumvented its purpose. The Realtor may not realize that you may have other programs to benefit their customer. You can compromise by designing a balanced sheet: list your programs, but don't go into detail.

The flexibility and volatility of rates create some interesting questions, and a marketing dilemma. Rates can change at the drop of a hat. You wait in the office several hours for rates, create a sheet, make 300 copies, and drive an hour to your territory to distribute them. What happens when rates change when you get there? Should you put a note on each one? No. Distribute the sheets. Your sheets must state clearly, "Pricing subject to change without notice."

What if rates are going down? Will you lose business? What about the existence of overages and underages on rate sheets? Should there be conformity in each mortgage branch? Should you instruct your processor, receptionist, and coworkers not to give information in conflict with the sheets you've distributed?

Distribution

We've already mentioned that originators typically hand-carry rate sheets throughout their territory. This is only one option. Mailings are good for high-volume originators who find it difficult to get out on the street but want their agents to be up-to-date on rates and programs.

The growth in popularity of facsimile machines presents another opportunity. What about faxing rates to key accounts? Ironically, faxed messages usually get more attention than those delivered personally.

Automation has already made its mark in the area of rate communication. Many local Boards of Realtors and other organizations have services that list rates via computer. In practice, the computer route hasn't made much of an impact. As with rate sheets, you must make a call to get the most up-to-date information before a contract is presented.

Producing and Distributing Newsletters

Provide Realtors with mortgage finance updates. For example, if FHA passes a rule requiring a larger downpayment, put the word out on the street.

Mortgage companies commonly produce newsletters tailored to Realtors. But consistency is a problem. If the corporate office of a large company produces the newsletter, it may overlook local topics and concerns. Further, employee turnover makes localized editions hard to produce in the long run.

The newsletter is an excellent tool to generate name recognition for yourself and introduce programs without producing and distributing rate sheets and flyers. It also gives you a reason to visit or send mail to an office.

What topics might you include in a newsletter? FHA, VA, Fannie Mae, and Freddie Mac changes head the list. Secondary market updates are also important, as Realtors are always hungry for information regarding interest rates and the overall economy. Collect local and national real estate news from trade journals. Include a discussion of generalized sales training or announcements for upcoming seminars. The list of possible topics is endless.

There are two variations on the newsletter as a marketing tool. One is to contribute to established Realtor newsletters. Many Realtors mail to or "farm" their territories, and can always use timely bits of information of interest to their homebuying market. Another variation is writing a newsletter to help Realtors sell. There are services available that enable originators to personalize a professionally prepared newsletter.

With today's word processing software you can produce a professional result in just a few hours from start to finish. You can photocopy the finished product with your business card as you would with rate sheets. Use colored paper for eye-catching, attractive results.

Writing Articles for Outside Publications

Many real estate trade groups publish monthly or quarterly publications. Editors are in search of good material and may even be willing to pay for it. Why not step forward? It's an excellent way to spread your name.

You can include your magazine, newspaper articles, and referrals in your marketing book. Realtors will perceive you as a person of knowledge and experience if you show them articles you wrote for a publication their organization produces.

Producing and Distributing Finance Guides for Homebuyers

Realtors can win homebuyers' loyalty by giving them educational materials such as finance guides. You, of course, supply the goods. Realtors distribute finance guides to clients through the mails and while doing relocations, open houses, and trade shows, or at one-on-one meetings.

Keep the guide brief and simple to suit a broad range of audiences. Organizations such as the Mortgage Bankers Association of America, Fannie Mae, and private mortgage insurance companies have educational materials you can purchase, personalize, and distribute. For example, Fannie Mae publishes a brochure on the 20-year mortgage which can be personalized with the mortgage company's name.

Producing and Distributing Finance Manuals for Realtors

Realtors will use mortgage company finance manuals as a resource only if they are complete, accurate, and routinely updated. To achieve this, the material requires periodic, tedious updating. Annual publication is an expensive alternative.

Your finance manual may take several forms. Pocket-sized versions are easy to handle and may be cheap to produce, but can include only limited information. For example, it's difficult to reduce federal tax charts.

Looseleaf notebooks are good for routine updating, but the cost of a notebook may exceed printing costs, and turnover in the real estate industry may interfere with organizing an update system. It may be more efficient to produce a new version each year, using the least expensive printing method. For example, you can staple together publications of up to eighty or ninety pages, using a heavy paper cover.

Defray costs by selling advertising to real estate servicers. Mortgage and real estate companies work closely with settlement agents, insurance companies, and pest control firms. Since your mortgage company refers business to these companies, they'll be responsive to an offer to advertise in your manual.

Basic Sales Tools

Basic sales tools are miscellaneous items that don't fit into the categories we've covered.

Business Cards. For originators, the business card is the most used introduction and networking tool. Give Realtors your business card the first time you meet them. Give them out at social gatherings and to clients when you ask for referrals. You'll be surprised at the increased business levels you achieve when every friend and every friend's friend knows what you do for a living.

An easy way to spread the word is to give extra cards to every applicant and Realtor. Remember to do this and you'll pass out hundreds each year. If one card in ten results in a loan application, the result is 10 percent more business.

How do you want them to remember you? Do you want your full and formal name listed? What do you want them to call you? If you have a professional designation such as CPA or CMB, include it. This is a way of conveying your qualifications in addition to the introductory package or letter we discussed earlier. Also, it's a good way to start a substantive discussion. For example, if you are a CPA, Realtors might want to discuss tax deductions and closing costs with you. Any conversation piece is valuable to you when you meet a client for the first time.

Originators use all kinds of titles. If you perused business cards throughout the industry, you would encounter such titles as: Financial Representative, Mortgage Banker, Banker, Loan Counselor, Financial Counselor, Account Representative, Builder Representative, and Loan Agent. You never know which of these titles are official as originators often tailor their titles to their target markets.

If you have something useful printed on the back of your card, Realtors will be more likely to keep it. Things you might have printed include principal and interest payment tables and information needed for loan application. Which phone numbers should you include on your card? Should you list your car phone number, or will the incoming calls be too expensive? Do you want to list your fax number?

Of course, Realtors need your home phone number. You may include a rate hotline number to cut down on calls from rate shoppers. If your rate sometimes differs from your company's published rates, leave the hotline number off. Also, you may not want applicants calling you at home for status checks. It's a good idea to have at least two different card designs for different types of clients.

Thank-You Notes and Cards

As business cards can be transformed from mundane business implements to dynamic sales tools, so can thank-you notes or cards. Thank-you notes are, quite simply, short, handwritten letters of thanks. Send thank-you notes:

- After meeting a sales agent or manager.
- To the listing and sales agent after they send a loan your way.
- To the applicant after settlement.
- To the settlement agent after settlement.
- To training class or seminar attendees.
- To a potential applicant after a prequalification.

Thank-you notes range from store-bought stationery to preprinted cards with your company logo or your name. Thank-you cards are typically foldovers or simple postcards.

Novelties

Pens, pencils, sunglasses, balloons, calendars, pads, visors, cups, stamps, and luggage tags are just a few examples of the thousands of items you might have printed with your name or company logo. Again, the trick here is to provide something Realtors will use. This requires a little more thought in selecting and designing a novelty.

Pens and pencils are useful, so Realtors keep them. Pads are also useful, but can be made even more so by printing information on them such as factors, prequalification tables or charts, or a listing questionnaire. What about a pad designed for cars or for calculator pockets?

Desk calendars are effective because they're on the Realtor's desk for a year. Printing helpful information on calendars might keep Realtors from "round filing" your calendar, as yours is one of many they receive each year. Include factors, phone numbers, and a list of items required for loan application.

Be careful about the value of gifts you give as they could be considered kickbacks. Focus on small items such as candy dishes for Realtors' offices that you keep filled, or providing doughnuts at sales meetings, tickets to an event, or a bottle of Champagne for the agent and borrower at settlement. You might even have a special label made to commemorate settlement. Send flowers to an agent who refers business to you. Take them to lunch.

With some thought and consistency, gifts can become an integral part of an overall sales strategy. A lunch here, some candy there, and flowers once in a while won't increase business. But the originator who becomes known as the candy, flower, or Champagne person is making an impact. So is the originator who builds relationships with top agents by taking them to lunch regularly.

Ads

Place individual ads in newspapers or newsletters listing not just your company logo, but your own name and phone number. In what types of publications should you place your ad? In larger metropolitan areas, citywide papers may be too expensive. You may do better in a local publication that targets your geographic market.

Other possibilities include newsletters that cover specific targets such as ethnic groups (perhaps even foreign language newspapers), or a newsletter distributed by an organization to which you belong. Local Boards of Realtors publish newsletters, and individual real estate firms produce small publications for prospective homeowners.

Your ads may vary in sophistication. You may simply publish your business card or use an ad your marketing department created. Don't include rates because deadlines will preclude an accurate and timely quote in smaller publications. Ads fall into the following categories:

- *Name identification ads.* These ads include your and your company's name and phone number, plus a list of a few of your products.

- *Product ads.* These promote and describe a specific product or products.

- *Service ads.* These advertise a particular service feature offered, such as five-day approvals.

- *Ads targeted to homeowners instead of Realtors.* These are more successful during periods of refinancing.

Products as Sales Tools

Program-oriented sales tools divert your target's focus from price. But an FHA mortgage is an FHA mortgage you say? Not when you can do them with 72-hour approvals. When you offer 72-hour approvals, the approval program sells mortgages. You may even take the idea a step further by offering pre-approval programs. Fast approval isn't your only tool for selling mortgage programs. Create buydowns that behave like ARMS. Programs offering rate cap protection rather than straight locks also present excellent sales opportunities.

The Marketing Book

A marketing book is a package of tools to help you market mortgages. Your book may be anything from a file folder with flyers to a complex financial software package you carry on the street to use with your laptop computer.

The contents of a marketing book include:

- Qualification materials

- Product comparison systems

- Preparation for loan application

- Specific product flyers

- Product feature background data

- References

- Introductory packages

Qualification materials. These are usually factor charts (most calculators can also handle that function), tax tables for FHA/VA qualification and rent equivalents, and pre-qualification or qualification charts.

Financial service software systems typically include a pre-qualification package for laptop PCs or even simpler computer systems. Product comparison systems compare rates over time, amortization progress, interest paid over time, and other factors. Financial comparison systems may also take the form of a simple chart, for example, one which compares a Growing Equity Mortgage rate of payment and amortization to a Fixed Rate. Others may be charts comparing worst case scenarios for Adjustable Rate Mortgages, and rent equivalents. While charts can be useful, these tools are static and can't be adjusted immediately for start rate and loan size.

Sophisticated loan application software technology is making many traditional origination tools obsolete. The same laptops that can be used to prequalify and sell products are being used to input loan application data. Yet, no matter what form of application tool you use, the applicant must be prepared. *The key to sales is service and the key to service is a good complete loan application. The key to a complete loan application is a prepared applicant.* While it is imperative that you contact the applicant personally to detail the required materials, you should take a few preliminary steps. Give the Realtor a list of application materials or a full application worksheet or workbook. Make sure the applicant gets these materials long before application.

Giving your clients a "preapplication kit" will save you and your company time and trouble. The following exhibit is one mortgage company's preapplication kit.

Exhibit 2-9:   Preapplication Kit

Dear Future Homeowner:

Thank you for considering ABC Mortgage as your mortgage lender. We believe that our "Easy App" mortgage lending concept offers the ultimate combination of convenience loan processing, speed and professionalism. ABC's professional approach to mortgage lending, which includes intense employee training, written rate confirmations with a guarantee, and educational materials such a our Homebuyers Finance Guide, is geared to give you the highest level of service possible.

The following "Pre Application Kit" notifies you of the specific information we will need to process your mortgage application. It also explains why this information is necessary.

If you take the "front end" time to thoroughly complete this questionnaire, we will return a prompt, professional evaluation of your loan. We'll ask that you bring certain items with you to the actual loan application which requires approximately 30-45 days to process. We will be sending your Realtor a status report weekly so that everyone is kept informed of the progress.

Very truly yours,

Dave Hershman
Executive Vice President

Exhibit 2-9   (Continued)

Borrower (Please provide pay stub covering the most current 30 days and last 2 year's W-2s)

1.   Name_____

Current Address_____

City_____State_____Zip_____Tel._____

Own_____Rent_____Date of Birth_____SS#_____

Yrs. at present address_____Yrs. of School_____Age____

Ages of Dependents_____,_____,_____,_____,_____,_____,_____

Marital Status: Married_____Single_____Unmarried_____

Note: If legally divorced or separated, a copy of the divorce or separation decree may be needed in evaluating your application.

If less than 2 yrs. at present address, please complete:

        Former Address_____Own_____Rent_____

        Former City_____State___Zip_____

2.   Employer_____

Address_____

City_____State_____Zip_____Tel._____

Hire date with present employer_____Title_____

Yrs. employed this line of work_____

Exhibit 2-9   (Continued)

    Monthly Income_____Salary_____Commission_____

    Bonus_____Overtime_____

    Alimony/Child Support_____

    Relocation Benefit Package_____

If less than 2 yrs. with current employer, please complete:

    Former Employer_____

    Address_____

    City_____State_____Zip_____Tel._____

    Employed from____to____Reason for Leaving_____

    Former Income_____Month____Title_____

Note: If you are self-employed or receive income from commissions or tips which will be used in qualifying, a signed photocopy of your personal (and corporate if applicable) federal income tax returns for the past two years will be needed. We will photocopy these documents for you. If you are self-employed, a year-to-date profit and loss statement and balance sheet from your accountant is also necessary. If you own over 25 percent of your corporation or partnership, you are considered self-employed.

Co-Borrower (Please provide pay stub covering the most current 30 days and last 2 year's W-2s)

1.   Name_____

    Current Address_____

    City_____State_____Zip_____Tel._____

    Own____Rent____Date of Birth____SS#_____

    Yrs. at present address_____Yrs. of School_____Age____

Exhibit 2-9   (Continued)

Ages of Dependents_____,_____,_____,_____,_____,_____,_____

Marital Status: Married_____Single_____Unmarried_____

Note: If legally divorced or separated, a copy of the divorce or separation decree may be needed in evaluating your application.

If less than 2 yrs. at present address, please complete:

Former Address_____Own_____Rent_____

Former City_____State___Zip_____

2.   Employer_____

Address_____

City_____State_____Zip_____Tel._____

Hire date with present employer_____Title_____

Yrs. employed this line of work_____

Monthly Income_____Salary_____Commission_____

Bonus_____Overtime_____

Alimony/Child Support_____Relocation Benefit Package_____

If less than 2 yrs. with current employer, please complete:

Former Employer_____

Address_____

City_____State_____Zip_____Tel._____

Employed from_____to_____Reason for Leaving_____

Former Income_____Month___Title_____

Exhibit 2-9   (Continued)

Note: If you are self-employed or receive income from commissions or tips which will be used in qualifying, a signed photocopy of your personal (and corporate if applicable) federal income tax returns for the past two years will be needed. We will photocopy these documents for you. If you are self-employed, a year-to-date profit and loss statement and balance sheet from your accountant is also necessary. If you own over 25 percent of your corporation or partnership, you are considered self-employed.

Assets

This section is a list of your assets and liabilities. It's used as an aid in judging your ability to repay, as it allows ABC Mortgage to determine your present financial position. This section is extremely important, since verification by the financial institution of certain of these items listed will be necessary. We urge you to complete this with care, particularly as regards names and addresses of institutions as well as account numbers.

1. Bank Accounts. Please bring 3 most recent monthly statements for each.

a) Checking and "Now" accounts

Bank/Institution	Address (include zip)	Acct. #	Balance
1. _____	_____	_____	_____
2. _____	_____	_____	_____
3. _____	_____	_____	_____

Exhibit 2-9   (Continued)

b) Savings accounts, certificates of deposit, money market funds, etc.

	Bank/Institution	Address (include zip)	Acct. #	Balance
1.	_____	_____	_____	_____
2.	_____	_____	_____	_____
3.	_____	_____	_____	_____

Note: Gift funds must be verified in borrower's accounts prior to loan approval ("We have an approved gift from _____ .")

c) Stocks and bonds

	Name & Type of Security (Broker Name & Address, include zip)	# Shares	Net Value
1.	_____	_____	_____
2.	_____	_____	_____
3.	_____	_____	_____

d) Life Insurance

Face Value (Total)_____Cash Value (Total)_____

e) Real Estate Owned

	Address, include zip	Current Value	Mortgage Balance
1.	_____	_____	_____
2.	_____	_____	_____
3.	_____	_____	_____

Note: If you own a rental property, we will need a copy of the current lease and 2 years' tax returns.

Exhibit 2-9   (Continued)

Liabilities

a) Loans, charge accounts, credit cards, revolving credit & other debts
(including stock pledges)—please bring most recent statements.

Bank or Creditor	Address (include zip)	Description-Acct.# (ex. Visa-4211-935-074-8-3)	Monthly Pmt.	Bal.
1.				
2.				
3.				
4.				
5.				
6.				
7.				
8.				

b. Real estate mortgages or landlord—please bring 12 months' cancelled
checks

Mortgage Holder or Landlord	Address (include zip)	Acct. #	Monthly Pmt.	Bal.
1.				
2.				
3.				

Note: Include any mortgage that has been "paid off" within the last 12
months (attach settlement sheet).

Exhibit 2-9   (Continued)

Miscellaneous Details

Please provide us with the following miscellaneous details of your purchase, all of which will eventually be needed after your loan has been granted.

1. Purchase price of subject property
    or estimated value.   _____

2. Amount of mortgage requested.   _____

3. Name of present owner.   _____

4. Your settlement agent's name & phone.   _____

5. Real estate agent's name & phone.   _____

6. Your homeowners insurance agent's
    name & phone.   _____

7   Estimated closing date.   _____

8. Subject property monthly cost data
    (if no listing provided).   _____

    a. Annual property taxes.   _____

    b. Estimated monthly homeowners ins.   _____

    c. Monthly cost of private mortgage
        insurance (if needed).   _____

    d. Approximate cost of utilities/month.   _____

9. Relocation package detailing company
    benefits.   _____

Exhibit 2-9   (Continued)

Information Needed for Loan Application

A. Provided by the Agent:

    1. Copy of the ratified contract.

    2. Any ratified addenda.

    3. A copy of the listing card.

    4. Copy of earnest money deposit check (should be certified or cashier's check).

B. Personal Information:

    1. Full names of all purchasers as they are to appear on the title.

    2. Social security numbers of all purchasers. Social security and picture identification for FHA loans.

    3. Present residence address for all purchasers.

    4. Previous address for all purchasers going back two years if they have not resided in the present home for two years.

    5. Home and office phone numbers.

C. Employment Information:

    1. Present employer name and address and a contact person to send employment verification form.

        a. Explanation for any gap during two-year history.

        b. Relocation letter for any transfers—giving date, salary, change location, and any relocation benefits.

    2. Previous employer's name and address and contact person going back two years if not in present job two full years.

    3. Present Salary. Year-to-date pay stub and last two years' W-2s.

Exhibit 2-9 (Continued)

4. If any variable income (commission, part-time income, bonus, overtime, interest income, etc.) is being used to qualify: two years' signed federal tax returns and W-2s and/or 1099s.

5. If self-employed: two years' signed federal individual and corporate returns (if there are corporate returns). Also a year-to-date profit and loss and balance sheet.

6. Diploma or transcript if student during two-year period.

D. Other income:

1. Rental income. Copy of a lease which is current and at least one year in length.

2. Alimony and child support. Only if used for qualification. Copy of divorce decree and property settlement (ratified) setting out terms. Proof of payment will also be requested at application.

3. Income from notes held. A copy of the ratified note and tax returns if interest was reportable during previous calendar year.

4. Retirement, social security, and disability income. Copy of award letter and latest check showing amount of present payment. Copy of end of the year statement if applicable. Social security income will be reported on tax returns.

E. Assets:

1. Bank accounts. Name of bank, address, account numbers, type of accounts and present balances. With checking use average balance. Copy of three most recent statements for all accounts.

Exhibit 2-9   (Continued)

2. Stocks and bonds. Copy of certificates or copy of recent (within 30 days) broker statement listing the holdings. Copy of statement can be used for many mutual funds, etc.

3. Life insurance. Cash value only if being used for down payment.

4. Vehicles. Year, make and value. Copy of the title if under four years old with no outstanding lien.

5. Real estate. Address and market value. If free and clear, deed of release, deed, or proof of mortgage payoff.

6. Present home. Copy of sales contract, settlement sheet, and/or lease.

7. Gift letter. Form will be provided by loan officer. Donor capacity must be verified. Receipt of funds must be shown in account.

F. Liabilities:

1. Credit cards. Account number and outstanding balance and most recent statement.

2. Loans. Auto, mortgage, personal, student, etc. Name of institution, address, account numbers, outstanding balance, monthly payment, months left on loan. Copy of payment coupon or statement. 12 months' statements or cancelled checks for all present mortgages.

3. Alimony and child support. Copy of ratified decree and property settlement setting out terms.

Exhibit 2-9   (Continued)

G. VA Loans:

   1. Certificate of eligibility. To obtain certificate, will need a DD-214 (Separation of Service) or, if in service, will need statement of service signed by Commanding Officer or Personnel Officer (certificate must be updated before application).

   2. If in service, may need authorization to live off base (DD Form 1747 from Housing Office) and transfer orders (if applicable).

H. Payments made at application:

   1. Application fee. $250 FHA/VA (includes cost of appraisal and credit report up to these amounts). $300 for conventional.

   2. One-half of one percent of the loan amount will be collected at application for refinances to be credited at settlement.

I. Present Home:

   1. Listing.

   2. Sales contract.

   3. Settlement sheet (if sold within last year).

   4. Name and address of present landlord.

   5. Deed & deed of trust (refinances only).

Specific product flyers. Your marketing book should include flyers featuring products you sell. These allow you to react to any sales situation. For example, you're handing out rate sheets to Realtors. Upon reading the sheet, they note that the figures don't address the specific needs of the customers with whom they're now working:

> "The people I'm taking out this weekend are looking at new homes that won't be delivered for six months."

> "Here's some information on our long term cap program. The cap program can offer rate protection up to six months in the future. The specifics are detailed on the flyer, but let's go over them so you fully understand how the program works."

Using plastic or acetate sheets in your marketing book allows you to put five to ten flyers in each page. This way each flyer is visible and you have extra copies to distribute. You are prepared to handle any sales situation, in a professional manner with sales tools, rather than having to say, "I have the material in the car or office—I'll get right back to you."

Product feature background data. Product feature data reinforces product sales flyers. This background data may include a variety of materials: a history of ARM indices, newspaper articles on the direction of rates or housing prices, relative strengths of savings institutions, and the tax advantages of maximum loan amounts. If you're presenting a flyer or argument in favor of (or against) an adjustable rate mortgage, back your case with charts, graphs, articles, or other data.

References. A point Jack Davis stresses in his sales seminars is the need for legitimate references to overcome objections. These reference letters may be from previous applicants or Realtors with whom you have done business. Perhaps these references concern your company—its strength and stability or service record. As unstable as the industry is, company stability and performance is a major concern of your clients. Again, using plastic sheets in the marketing book allows you to present one copy or several copies for easy access and distribution.

Introductory packages. A full-scale introductory package introducing you and your company might include a letter of reference, resume, and a company description or brochure. Deliver these individually or in a package or folder. Use these introductory packages for cold calls on offices, meetings with office managers or builders, or every time you meet a new Realtor.

Developing a Mailing List

An originator mailing list is a powerful tool for office penetration, securing key Realtor accounts, and as part of a broader networking strategy. The ideal format for the list is on word processing or database software coded by category, enabling you to print labels from all categories for mass mailings, or to select specific categories for targeted, personalized letters. Updating the list is simple on an automated system. If such an automated system is unavailable, you can maintain a manual database by storing names and addresses in label form and photocopying them for each mailing.

List Components:

    Real Estate Category
        All Realtors in offices you visit.
        All Realtors in the geographic territory you cover.
        Managers in real estate offices you solicit.
        All Realtors (listing and selling) for whom you have originated a loan.
        Top producers in the territory.
        Builders in the territory.
        Realtor subcategories.
- Realtors who work with relocation.
- Realtors who work with buyers.
- Realtors who work with sellers.
- Realtors who specialize in condominium complexes.
- Realtors who specialize in new homes.
- Realtors who have attended your seminars.

Business-related network category
    Settlement agents.

    Insurance agents.

    Financial planners.

    CPAs.

    Appraisers.

    People in any profession that come into contact with a large
    volume of homebuyers.

General public category
    Previous mortgage applicants.

    Any ethnic, religious, social or other group to which you have
    ties.

    Groups in your neighborhood or origination territory, such as
    your condominium association or PTA.

    Other mortgage originators.

    All other personal contacts (friends, colleagues).

Possible Mailings
    General mailout (non-personalized, to all on list).
        • A regular newsletter on mortgage finance.
        • Introductory letter or package (if you are new in the
          business or with a new company).
        • Specific program flyers.
        • Rate sheets.
        • A recent article about real estate values and/or finance.

    Targeted mailout.
        • Personalized letters to any specific group—asking for
          referrals, meetings, and introducing programs.
        • To Realtors—invitations to finance seminars, follow-up
          to loan applications.
        • To public—invitation to homebuyers' seminar.
        • To top agents—rates sheets, program flyers, personal-
          ized message about service.
        • To business-related groups—programs that may help
          their group and increase their business. For example,

program of self-insurance to maximize deductions to financial planners.

- Follow-up letter after closing.
- Refinance mailing to previous applicants or home-owners' association.
- Status sheets to Realtors.

Forms of mailouts.

- Actual letters mailed in envelopes.
- Preprinted postcard.
- Thank-you cards.
- One-piece mailers.

The following exhibit is an example of such a mailing list.

Exhibit 2-10: Sample Alphabetized/Coded Mailing List

John Richards
Manager
Mt. Realty
Real Place, VA 12345
MG

Susan Lamont
Mt. Realty
Real Place, VA 12345
PR

Joseph Fisher
Valley Realty
Real Place, VA 12345
RL

Edward Stastiny
Financial Planning T
Fake Place, VA 12346
FP

Joyce Troutman
23 Forest Lane
Lost Forest, VA 12348
PE

Codes: MG = Manager
        PR = Presidents Club
        RL = Realtor
        FP = Financial Planner
        PE = Personal

You might use a thank-you card to send to Realtor(s) and/or applicants after each loan application or closing, or use postcards for individual notes such as "I enjoyed lunch last week" or such preprinted messages as "Rates have come down to nine and one-half percent—the time to refinance is now!"

Compose newsletters, rate sheets, and flyers so that they can be folded and affixed with mailing labels. This saves the expense of envelopes for repetitious mass mailings.

The following exhibits include examples of mailings for a variety of purposes.

Exhibit 2-11: Sample Targeted Letter

ABC Mortgage Company
Podunk, Virginia 12346

March 1, 1989

Sue Realtor
123 Realty Company
Broker Haven, Virginia 12347

Dear Sue:

Springtime is rapidly approaching. Listings are starting to show on the boards and soon the purchasers will emerge from their winter hibernation.

Sue, I know that you are the area specialist in military relocations. This is why I thought of you first when ABC Mortgage decided to release its "get a loan up front" program. Under this program, we now have the ability to approve your VA purchasers before they buy the house.

Think of how much time and effort it would save you to have your incoming clients approved for a certain loan amount before they come into town in search of a home. You may then direct them to the homes in a certain price range, negotiate with strength, and go to settlement very quickly.

Lets get together next week to discuss the implementation of such a system, Sue. I will call you in a few days.

Sincerely,

Opportunity Knocks
Originator

Exhibit 2-12: Sample Targeted Letter

ABC Mortgage Company
Podunk, Virginia 12345

March 1, 1989

Don Mortgaged
123 New House
New Neighborhood, Virginia 12347

Dear Don:

Congratulations! I spoke with Ed, your settlement agent, and Marty, your agent. Both indicated that closing was as smooth as silk.

Don, I couldn't be prouder of the fact that I was able to assist you in purchasing your dream house. Because it's your first home, I know it must be special. It's transactions such as these that make me realize my job is special.

If you know of anyone else who is about to purchase a home, please let me know. I am enclosing a few extra cards for your use. I really appreciate your assistance in contacting acquaintances I may serve.

I will call in a few days to see if you have any follow-up questions. Once again, Don, thanks for the chance to serve you.

Sincerely,

Much Richer
Originator

cc: Ed Agent
    Marty Realtor

Exhibit 2-13: Sample General Letter

ABC Mortgage Company
Podunk, Virginia 12345

Dear Friend:

On Tuesday, March 27, the Veterans Administration announced the lowering of the maximum rate for VA loans to 9 1/2 percent, effective the following day. This is the first time we've seen single digit rates for over a year. Just a few months ago, we were financing homes at 12 percent. The time to move into a fixed rate or to a lower fixed rate is now! If you are ready to discuss the possibilities of a refinance to lower your payments, move to a safer loan, take cash out or discuss any other question, give me a call at 444-4444. It would be wise to do so before the Spring rush begins. Most of the time we can accomplish your goals with no cash from your pocket and with a minimum of paperwork. I look forward to working with you in the near future.

Sincerely,

Lewis Getem
Originator

Exhibit 2-14: Introductory Letter

Rob Sellars
The Akin Co. Real Estate—BH&G
255 W. Foothill Blvd., Ste. 100
Upland, CA 91786

Dear Rob,

I would like to take this opportunity to introduce myself to you. My name is John Terveer and the company for which I work is Superior Service Mortgage. I am the Loan Officer for the area in which your office is located.

You will find that business is conducted differently here. We don't annoy you with unscheduled appointments, ask for loans, or clutter up your desk with rate sheets. We provide you with the latest in real estate sales tools to help you increase your production. Plain and simple. The benefit to you is a professional relationship that you can bank on.

Enclosed you will find a sample of one of our sales tools. We have prepared a workbook for you with all of the sales tools that we provide. I would like to present your workbook to you and explain the different tools that it contains. I will contact you to set up an appointment that is convenient for both of us.

I look forward to meeting you. I know that you will be pleased when you find yourself closing more escrows each month. I know you will be pleased with the professional service you receive.

Sincerely,

John Terveer

Exhibit 2-15: Preferred Realtor Letter

Dear Preferred Realtor:

Jersey Shore Savings and Loan Association is testing a special program for selected Preferred Brokers. This program, designed especially for the real estate professional, will feature:

- Expert Processing
- Faster Service
- Common Sense Underwriting
- Dependable Status Reports

This special program will be available for the next 120 days on single family primary residences. As an inducement to try it we will refund the $300.00 application fee to your client at closing. We will also pay for the appraisal and credit investigation.

At the end of the trial period, we will invite you to meet with the people who made the program a success to discuss additional ways to make this service better for you.

We at Jersey Shore feel that you owe it to yourself and your clients to try this innovative program, not once but many times during the trial period. In that way you will see why we are known as "YOUR MORT-GAGE CAPITAL."

Sincerely,

Walter Rissmeyer,
Loan Originations Manager

Exhibit 2-16: Recently Sold Properties

Dear_____:

Congratulations on another _____(company name) sold sign at _____(address). The mark of a thorough real estate professional is to continue a full-time marketing effort to achieve a sale. Congratulations on another sale.

Although I've worked in this particular marketing area for _____, we have never had the opportunity to work together. I realize that meeting "another loan officer" may not be at the top of your priority list. However, I am not "just another loan officer!" The only way you can verify that statement is to invest a few minutes of your time to find out.

I'll be calling you on _____ to arrange a 15- to 20-minute convenient meeting time.

I look forward to calling you on _____.

Respectfully,

Exhibit 2-17: Initial Request (Letter Form) to Broker

Date

Broker's Name
Company
Address

Dear_____:

Many different Realtors have recently shared with me the fact that they have more loan officers walking into their offices than they have properties to sell. This has proven to be an inconvenience for many of the Realtors with whom I've recently spoken.

I don't believe I deserve your business unless I earn it! Any lender can come in and take applications, but I seriously believe my job is to work with your agents to create applications. I realize the competition for the real estate dollar is as great for you as the competition for mortgage dollars is for me. In order to earn your business, I must do what I can to assist _____ corporate goals.

I am, therefore, writing to you because I've developed a short presentation on_____(general overview and why it would be valuable).

I don't know whether or not you perceive this suggestion to be a "value added" service for your company, but I would appreciate the opportunity to prove that it is. If you feel your agents could use a shot in the arm with suggestions that would increase their commissions and your earnings, I'd like to speak to your group.

I look forward to contacting you within the next seven days to discuss the action steps necessary to make this idea a reality. As always, my desire is not simply to meet your expectations, it's to exceed them.

Respectfully,

Exhibit 2-18: Newspaper Announcements

Dear_____(first name):

Congratulations on your recent recognition as a top producer for _____. If your adulthood scrapbook is anything like mine, I thought you might enjoy having another copy of the newspaper article.

Although I am the [one of the] leading producers in my office, we have not yet had the opportunity to work together. Because I believe success should be by design and not by accident, I'll be calling you within the next three days to arrange a time we can meet. Thirty minutes to discuss the formation of a mutually beneficial business relationship is a warranted ideal!

Once again, congratulations on a job well done! I look forward to speaking with you before the end of the week.

Respectfully,

Exhibit 2-19: Recently Listed Properties

Dear _____ :

Congratulations on having accepted the marketing responsibility for the property located at_____.

Although there are myriad financing opportunities available for purchasers of that particular property, I have a few ideas that could decrease your marketing time.

 I will call you _____ to arrange a convenient time we can get together.

My goal is not simply to meet your expectations, it's to exceed them. With that goal in mind, I look forward to contacting you _____.

Respectfully,

Exhibit 2-20: Refinance Target Letter

American Residential Mortgage Corporation
2 Pidgeon Hill Dr., Suite 300, Sterling, VA 22170
Telephone: 703-450-4900

American Residential Mortgage Corporation, a leader in the mortgage lending field, is pleased to extend the benefits of our Streamlined Refinance Program to you.

American Residential Mortgage Corporation is one of the top ten mortgage bankers in the nation with $3.2 billion in originations in 1989. American Residential has the capacity to offer diversified programs at competitive rates with excellent service.

As interest rates fall back into the low- to-mid nines, increasing numbers of homeowners are abandoning their escalating adjustable-rate mortgages (many of which are at, or will soon be at 11 percent or greater) for a fixed-rate mortgage in the low nines with no out-of-pocket expense!

For example, a one year ARM originated in August 1987, at 8 3/4 percent would have taken an annual increase of 2 percent each year.

> year 1 $150,000 @ 8 3/4% = $1,180 per mo.
> year 2 $150,000 @ 10 3/4% = $1,400 per mo.
> year 3 $150,000 @ 12 3/4% = $1,630 per mo.

Stop!!

Refinance to 9 1/2 percent fixed and save $370 per month.

years 1-30 $150,000 @ 9 1/2% = $1,260 per mo.

Exhibit 2-20   (Continued)

How much money will I save by refinancing my current mortgage?

To illustrate the monthly savings by reducing your current interest rate:

The loan amount is $150,000. Each 1 percent decrease in interest rate will save you $112. Therefore, if you have a current rate of 11 percent or higher, refinancing your mortgage down to a fixed rate of 9 1/2 percent could save you $200 or more every month!

Can I take cash out of the equity that I have accumulated?

Yes. You may find it advantageous to take cash out during your refinance. There is no limit to how much cash you choose to extract, as long as 20 percent equity remains in the property after closing. This money can be used to consolidate existing debt at a much lower rate, buy an automobile, or make home improvements and still deduct the interest for tax purposes!

What about my closing costs?

In nearly all cases, the closing costs can be rolled into the new loan amount—no out-of-pocket expense!

What items should I bring to loan application?

—Current "Deed of Trust"

—3 months' bank statements

—Last month's pay stub

—Last 2 years' W-2s

If your current rate is 11 percent or greater or you currently have an adjustable rate, you are paying too much money!

Exhibit 2-20   (Continued)

Whether refinancing your home to lower your mortgage rate and payment or taking equity out of your home to add home improvements, to
finance an automobile, or even to take a vacation, the time to act is now!
Virtually all fees can be covered within the new loan amount, with no
out-of-pocket expense.

For more information on American Residential's Streamline Refinance
Program, I can be reached at (703) 450-4900.

Sincerely,

Anthony Mills
Loan Officer

Exhibit 2-21: Introductory Letter

Thomas Morgan
Branch Manager, American Residential Mortgage
Service
Education
Price & Product
Here's American Residential!

What is American Residential Mortgage?

American Residential Mortgage was formed in 1983 as a subsidiary of Imperial Savings and Loan. When First Nationwide Bank purchased American Residential in January of 1988, it had already grown into one of the largest lenders in the nation with over $4 billion in annual mortgage production.

First Nationwide was purchased by Ford Motor Company as part of its expansion into Financial Services. First Nationwide has become the Nation's second largest savings institution with unmatched financial strength under Ford leadership.

All American Residential employees possess unique attributes which bring them to our team. Our clients receive the benefits of experience beyond the realm of mortgage banking, whether this experience consists of a legal background or experience with secondary marketing conduits like Freddie Mac. We feel this plays a part in what we consider to be the most conscientious mortgage processing available in the industry.

We have learned that success in Mortgage Banking is the result of long hours of work and a commitment to the bottom line—getting loans closed! Our philosophy asks, "What good is a great price or product if you can't deliver?"

I hope the following package will help to explain how American Residential implements its philosophy and how we are developing a reputation for providing the highest level of service in the Washington Metropolitan Area.

Exhibit 2-21   (Continued)

Price & Product

Many Realtors believe that price is the single most important criteria when selecting a mortgage lender. In fact, price is a crucial aspect of providing good service. But rate sheets—the advertisement flyers which many lenders distribute—can often be misleading. As advertisements, they are designed to get the Realtor's attention. A closer look, however, reveals phrases like "SUBJECT TO CHANGE WITHOUT NOTICE" or "RATE AND POINTS DETERMINED AT APPLICATION." This makes assisting a buyer in finding a competitive mortgage product almost impossible.

Announcing a Revolution in Rate Lock Options

Your clients can always get the lowest rate available!

If you watch mortgage rates, you will notice that rates do two things— they go up and they go down. Today's best rate lock quote could be unacceptable to a borrower if, between application and settlement, market rates improve. The result? Lost time (because the case will be transferred to another lender) and unhappy customers ("why won't they give me the lower rates?"). We have a happy answer.

With American Residential you can ALWAYS get the lower rate!

From now on you can write a financing contingency clause that reads: "RATE SHALL BE TODAY'S MARKET RATE, OR THE RATE IN EFFECT AT CLOSING, **WHICHEVER IS LOWER!**"

WE ALSO OFFER ONE OF THE WIDEST PRODUCT MENUS AVAILABLE:

80 Percent No income	1, 3, 7 Year ARMS	Fixed to 5MM
Builder Commitments	90, 120, 180 Day Caps	Direct Endorsement
Low Point Buydowns	Non-approved Condos	72 Hour Approval
VHDA	Trailing Spouse	15, 20, 25, 30 Yr Am
Balloon Programs	15 Minute Preapproval	No Points/Fees
Investor Loans	Compressed 3-2-1	2nd Homes

Exhibit 2-21   (Continued)

Education

The cornerstone of American Residential's philosophy is education. Each member of American Residential's staff, whether a loan officer, processor or underwriter, is initiated with a rigorous training period before assuming any individual responsibilities. Additionally, all staff participate in periodic supplemental or continuing training to update on our continual changing business or to cover areas not previously taught.

We believe it's equally important for Realtors to gain the knowledge they need to be confident and well-versed in residential real estate finance. To this end, we offer:

Residential Finance Manual. A highly regarded comprehensive guide and sourcebook. Available through our training seminars.

Training Classes for Realtors. We offer basic and in-depth classes on topics ranging from qualification and loan products to self-employment or investment property financing. These classes are approved in Maryland and Washington for continuing education credit. We also offer brief update sessions to discuss developments in the mortgage lending industry.

Spot Consultation. We are always available to discuss any transaction and recommend a course of action that will speed your sale. Our loan officers have instant access to credit bureaus, underwriters, and managers to address your concerns.

Homebuyer's Finance Guide. Provided as a discussion and educational tool for prospective buyers. This tool also prepares applicants for the initial application interview.

We believe we are mortgage experts. There is no mystery to what we do. We simply pride ourselves on the best product knowledge and in our ability to share that knowledge to help you MAKE MORE SALES.

Call me for a training session anytime.

Exhibit 2-21 (Continued)

Service

The scariest thing a Realtor may face in recommending a mortgage lender is that once a loan application is taken, the process is out of their hands. Too often in this situation it's a week prior to a scheduled settlement when the parties are informed that crucial documentation was never requested or received by the lender, or that settlement documentation was not received, or when any of a host of unexpected problems arise.

American Residential's processing system does not allow this to happen. Within 48 hours of loan application:

- All verification requests are sent.
- The credit report and appraisal are ordered.
- The case is reviewed by a senior staff member or branch manager for adequacy in the areas of application documentation, borrower qualification and program guidelines.

Then:

Every Thursday, the loan officer and processor meet to go over all cases in process. Documentation is logged into the file and any deficiencies are addressed. Any documentation still outstanding is re-requested.

A copy of the status log is delivered to all interested parties each week.

You never have to be in the dark again.

HOW DOES THIS HELP **YOUR** BUSINESS?

When the buyer calls, you show *your* service excellence by *knowing* the status of the loan! You can coordinate closing, confirm rates, check deadlines—*you're in control!*

We can't drop the ball on a case—when you use American Residential, you're on the team!

Exhibit 2-21   (Continued)

We also offer the following services:

- Open House Spreadsheets—show buyers how much they can buy.
- Quick Pre-Approvals mean your sellers can have confidence when they accept *your* contingent contract.
- Branch Managers have underwriting authority.
- 24-hour service—we are always available to meet your needs.

Enclose your resume and your objective — superior customer service.

Technology as a Selling Tool

"High tech" has reached every facet of the mortgage industry. We receive mortgage insurance commitments via computer or fax machine, and take applications on laptop computers. We link FHA appraisals and credit reports electronically. This proliferation of equipment creates the opportunity to expand our repertoire of sales techniques. The following is a list of machines we should be using to generate sales, and ways to use them.

Computer

Financial comparison software compares qualification requirements, rates over time, payments over time, and amortization progress for different loan programs. Portable computers and printers allow you to enter information as the Realtor or potential purchaser gives it to you—a real time-saver.

Another software program related to financial product comparison systems compares listing data. You can compare the subject property with several mortgage programs available for financing its purchase, focusing on income needed to qualify and required cash. The following exhibits are examples of such spreadsheets.

Computers can do more than compare mortgage programs. The ability to input application data directly for transmittal to a processing location speeds processing and approval time. You may generate status reports or order verifications, appraisals, and credit reports at the touch of a button. The resulting high level of service and resulting customer satisfaction will differentiate you from your competitors.

You can also use computers to create sales tools—flyers, rate sheets, and presentations. The evolution of desktop publishing and high-quality printers has given originators the ability to produce professional-looking sales materials. Word processing software allows you to create newsletters, and we have already discussed the role of computers for mailings.

Exhibit 2-22

 SUPERIOR SERVICE MORTGAGE
CORPORATION

```
               CONVENTIONAL FINANCING ALTERNATIVES
               ------------------------------------
                       -PROPERTY ADDRESS-
                       1524 N. MARJORIE
                       CLAREMONT, CA. 91711

               AGENT:    CHRIS TORCIVIA
              OFFICE:    CENTURY 21 GENE HART
       LISTING PRICE:    $230,000.00
```

	10% DOWN	10% DOWN	20% DOWN	20% DOWN
	ADJUSTABLE 6 MONTHS	ADJUSTABLE ANNUALLY	E-Z QUALIFIER ADJUSTABLE	30 YEAR FIXED
INTEREST RATE	8.500%	9.125%	8.625%	10.375%
POINTS	1.250	1.500	1.500	1.500
LOAN AMOUNT	$207,000.00	$207,000.00	$184,000.00	$184,000.00
PRIN. & INT.	$1,591.65	$1,684.22	$1,431.13	$1,665.95
PROP. TAXES	220.42	220.42	220.42	220.42
HAZARD INS.	40.00	40.00	40.00	35.00
PMI	$76.67	$76.67	0.00	0.00
MONTHLY PMT.	$1,928.73	$2,021.30	$1,691.55	$1,921.37
DOWN PAYMENT	$23,000.00	$23,000.00	$46,000.00	$46,000.00
POINTS IN $	2,587.50	3,105.00	2,760.00	2,760.00
APPROX CLOSING	1,800.00	1,800.00	1,700.00	1,700.00
IMPOUNDS	2,063.08	2,116.25	1,072.19	1,204.52
TOTAL CASH REQ.	$29,450.58	$30,021.25	$51,532.19	$51,664.52

```
             THE CLOSING COSTS AND IMPOUNDS ARE ESTIMATES.
             MONTHLY PROP. TAXES AND HAZARD INS.
             ARE OPTIONAL FOR 20% DOWN PROGRAMS.

                   CALL FOR PROGRAM INFORMATION.

        BRANCH MANAGER:_____

             JOHN TERVEER - (714) 981-1400
```

Exhibit 2-23

SS SUPERIOR SERVICE MORTGAGE
CORPORATION

```
           CONVENTIONAL FINANCING ALTERNATIVES
           -------------------------------------
                   -PROPERTY ADDRESS-
                   425 CENTER STREET
                   POMONA, CA.

        AGENT:    CHRIS TORCIVIA
        OFFICE:   CENTURY 21 GENE HART
 LISTING PRICE:   $165,000.00
```

****

	20% DOWN	
	FIXED	ADJUSTABLE
INTEREST RATE	12.750%	10.000%
POINTS	1.500	1.500
LOAN AMOUNT	$132,000.00	$132,000.00
PRIN. & INT.	$1,434.44	$1,158.39
PROP. TAXES	154.00	154.00
HAZARD INS.	35.00	35.00
PMI INS.	0.00	0.00
MONTHLY PMT.	$1,623.44	$1,347.39
DOWN PAYMENT	$33,000.00	$33,000.00
POINTS IN $	1,980.00	1,980.00
APPROX CLOSING	1,400.00	1,400.00
IMPOUNDS	2,031.64	1,882.47
TOTAL CASH REQ.	$38,411.64	$38,262.47

****

```
        THE CLOSING COSTS AND IMPOUNDS ARE ESTIMATES.

        THIS PROPERTY IS ZONED FOR COMMERCIAL USE.


 BRANCH MANAGER:_____

        JOHN TERVEER - (714)981-1400
```

Exhibit 2-24

PROPERTY ADDRESS: _____

315-424-0218 (24 Hr. Answering Service)   LISTING REALTOR NAME: _____
800-448-3200
1010 James Street   _____
Syracuse, New York 13203

DID YOU KNOW THAT???
You may purchase this home for a price of $ _____
The cash you will need to buy this home is only $ _____
Breakdown of the cash needed is:
$_____ Down payment*
$_____ Closing costs (includes____points)**
$_____ Prepayables (taxes, insurance, prepaid interest, 1st yr. PMI)

* Different down payment mortgages are also available - different figures will apply.
**Lesser or zero point loans are also available.

Your approximate monthly   Approximate annual gross income needed
payment based on: to qualify for this mortgage payment:

Loan Amt. _____w/ MIP $ _____
              Included (if FHA)

Interest Rate_____ %   This amount assumes monthly recurring debt
                                   payments of no more than:
P + I   _____
                                               $ _____
Taxes   _____

Fire Ins.   _____   TOTAL MONTHLY PAYMENT

PMI &/or Association   _____(Estimated)
Fees   _____

WANT TO KNOW MORE??? FOR AN ANALYSIS ON YOUR PERSONAL SITUATION CALL:

You can use the computer to access information to include in educational materials such as newsletters and articles. The Mortgage Banking Service Corporation (MBSC) ECHO system is linked to HUD and other government and quasi-governmental agencies. The system allows lenders to access and monitor pending legislation and regulations.

The existence of computers in real estate offices has presented the opportunity for "technologically direct" sales. Many organizations have integrated rate information from several lenders on one system. Several local boards of Realtors have accomplished such integration through Multiple Listing Service (MLS) data systems. Other companies have taken the concept a step further, combining many lenders' program data in one system. After a Realtor selects a program, an originator enters the application on-site, in the Realtor's office.

At least one software company is developing "judgment software." These programs enable mortgage companies to automate much of the underwriting function. The originator in the field inputs decision factors into a laptop computer and receives an answer without calling the underwriter.

Duplicating Equipment

Mortgage companies use copiers from origination to delivery, and couldn't function without them. Every mortgage office must have a high-quality copier. Copiers should be able to:

- Produce two-sided copies. You can use this feature to combine rate sheets with educational materials. For example, you can put information needed for loan application on the back of rate sheets.

- Reduce and enlarge. The ability to reduce and enlarge materials helps you produce high-quality sales materials. You can reduce pictures to fit on a rate sheet or program flyers. You can enlarge headlines for emphasis.

- Add a second color. More advanced machines are able to add another color (typically red, blue, or green). Materials printed in a color other than black appear professionally printed. Another way to incorporate a second color is to print rate sheet or flyer masters and make copies onto colored paper.

Other photocopier features useful for producing professional-looking sales materials include the ability to vary shades and collate. The machine must be reliable and able to produce clean copies consistently during periods of heavy use. Even the best material will be compromised by poor copy quality. Finally, in our quest for time management, a fast photocopier helps.

Facsimile Machines

Ten years ago a fax machine was a luxury. Now, every mortgage office has one. We receive rates and mortgage insurance commitments, and order credit reports and appraisals by fax as often as we do by computer. As more real estate offices acquire fax machines, you will be able to send rate sheets or status reports to a key agent or an entire office.

An experienced originator may have 10 or 20 key agents in separate offices. The fax machine allows you to transmit weekend rates instantly. As this method of transmission is still a novelty, it draws attention. That's why fax machines are useful to announce programs—your transmission gets attention.

Recording Equipment

With the small investment of a telephone answering machine, a mortgage company can set up a 24-hour rate hotline. Publish the hotline number on rate sheets, business cards, and in newspaper advertisements. But setting up a hotline creates a dilemma: while the hotline may save time by diverting "rate check" calls, you lose the opportunity to sell price-shopping clients on more than just price.

The following exhibit is a sample script for your rate hotline.

Exhibit 2-25: Rate Hotline Script

Welcome to ABC Mortgage Company's rate hotline. ABC Mortgage company is the leading lender in the Boston Metropolitan area and can service all your first trust mortgage needs, including FHA, VA, conventional conforming, and jumbo loans to $1,000,000. The following rates are in effect until noon the _____th. All points include the loan origination fee:

FHA and VA 30-year: _____% and _____
Conventional 30-year to $187,450:_____% and _____
Jumbo 30-year fixed to 750,000: _____% and _____
15-Year Growing Equity Program: _____% and _____
Our One Year ARM starts at: _____% and _____
Our Three Year ARM starts at: _____% and _____

For further information call 556-1212. All rates and points quoted are subject to change without notice.

Availability is key for any salesperson. You're "in the field" most of the day. Many real estate transactions are negotiated in the evening or on weekends. You must have a telephone answering machine at home, preferably with your office and pager number included in the announcement. Pagers have become standard tools for mortgage sales personnel. But pagers are becoming obsolete with the advent of voice mail systems that can page you and take a message simultaneously.

Car phones, answering machines for car phones, and portable phones are indispensable time management tools, and the latest models of portable phones are actually not much larger than a standard paging device.

Calculators

The calculator is no longer an instrument of basic math. The advanced machines that most Realtors and loan originators carry can calculate precise payments, amortization schedules, compounding, and truth-in-lending Annual Percentage Rates (APRs), and can perform complex calculations quickly. Be familiar with the calculators and functions your agents use. And be prepared to teach your clients how to use them. They'll thank you with loans.

3

Selling Through Seminars and Presentations

Public Speaking

You can't sell without a command of speech. Whether overcoming objections one-on-one, corralling the telephone rate shopper, or giving a seminar to one hundred Realtors, the difference between failure and mediocrity and success is your ability to use words to persuade. Speech is integral to salesmanship.

The Speech, Seminar, or Sales Meeting Presentation

Almost everybody fears public speaking. But public speaking is avoidable—unless you are a salesperson. Then, public speaking should be the main weapon in your arsenal.

What can public speaking do for you? You may spend months breaking into an office, having lunches with Realtors, and developing relationships. But with one electrifying presentation you can win an entire office of ten to one hundred Realtors.

Sounds simple? It isn't. No one becomes a good speaker overnight. It takes years of practice, and can't be learned by cramming. Dr. Roko Paskov, in his seminar *Confident Public Speaking*, clears up some common misconceptions.

> "There are no 'born good speakers.' Even experienced orators get stage fright. Though all are not created with the endowment of scintillating oratory skills, some are born (or raised) with a propensity to use verbal communication more than others."

Are these people the only ones who can become good public speakers or one-on-one salespersons? Not necessarily, because a person who talks constantly may be missing the listening component of sales. On the other hand, someone who is comfortable with speaking in general will be more likely to take the steps necessary to become a good speaker. These steps include talking at every opportunity in more non-threatening situations, such as sales or staff meetings. Volunteer to train new originators or introduce them around the office. Take another originator out "on the street." There are literally hundreds of opportunities to hone speaking skills—selling over the phone is a perfect non-threatening situation. Each day and situation brings you closer to the goal of effective public speaking.

As you move toward this goal, build capacity. Move from speaking up at meetings to making a short presentation on a success you had during the week. Because it was a personal success experience, you will be familiar with the topic and you will feel strongly about the topic. Then, as you move to short sales meetings for small groups of Realtors or training sessions for a few originators, you must learn the most important point of speaking: *listening.* Listening works symbiotically with speech to provide the real "knock-out punch" of any sales presentation.

Exhibit 3-1: Dr. Paskov's Confident Public Speaking— Major Points to Remember

1. Start small and work up. There is no quick and easy way.
2. Volunteer and practice. Start with a message important to you.
3. Prepare for contingencies.
4. Expect to get nervous. Turn that nervousness into positive energy.
5. The audience can't tell that you're nervous.
6. Assume success.
7. Familiarize yourself with the group. Circulate.
8. Smile before the audience.
9. Start deliberately, confidently, and slowly.
10. Use non-verbal skills. Use you hands, smile, lean forward.
11. Analyze the audience.
12. Set goals.
13. Plan.
14. Your opening must be a "grabber."
15. Speak conversationally—not too slowly.
16. Vary levels of speech.
17. Get rid of distractions: "um," "okay," other verbal tics.
18. Read aloud often. Record yourself.
19. Listen to others speaking.
20. Prepare to be impromptu.
21. Be appropriate. Avoid politics and religion.
22. Use the language, jargon for credibility. But don't speak over their heads.
23. Be vivid—people must understand the first time.
24. Use visual aids—87 percent of learning is visual. But don't distract.
25. Go over a performance checklist: facilities, tables, chairs, and something to write on.

Practice To speak effectively you must know the subject inside and out. You must practice alone out loud, with a tape recorder and in front of peers. The first time you give a three minute speech, practice it a hundred times before you present it.

Practice must go one step further: anticipation. Since part of any talk will involve questions and fluid situations, you must learn to anticipate. Perhaps you'll be given an extra five minutes more or less than you planned for. What questions will the audience ask?

If it's true there are a limited number of objections you'll meet while selling, then there are also a limited number of questions that will arise at a presentation. Practice responses as well as the speech itself.

Organize. Your presentation, whether three minutes or two hours, must be well-organized. To organize, you must first identify the goal of the presentation. See Exhibit 3-2 for sample goals.

Analyze. Audience analysis is the equivalent to listening in relationship sales. A smart presenter "sizes up" Realtors before, during, and after a speech. Are they lively or half asleep? Familiar or strangers? Rushed or relaxed? Conservative or a fun-loving office? Responsive or antagonistic? These observations should direct your approach, speed, language, and humor.

Elasticize. In what may sound a contradiction in terms, we told you to practice your speech again and again. Yet, the worst speech is one rigidly memorized and regurgitated. Knowing your material backward and forward so you can talk about it is your goal.

Know what to say about topics. Dr. Paskov advocates 3 x 5 cards with points that guide the presentation. Elaborate on each point with stories (flexibly embellished, dwelled upon, or skimmed over, using your audience analysis).

Use Humor. Humor is the main weapon of any public speaker. With good humor you can win an audience over, make a stolid topic bearable, and make any point memorable. You don't have to be a comedian to deliver a humorous presentation.

Bringing a funny story will do. Talk about originators, buyers, or even Realtors (tactfully!). Realtors will always laugh about originators or their travels, or learning the business. A little humor at the opening loosens up unfamiliar audiences.

Don't be afraid to use a story Realtors find funny time and time again. You may think it's old because you've repeated it ten times, but as long as the audience is new, it's the first time for most of them. Every time you hear something funny, write it down. If it's in a publication, cut it out and keep a joke or story file. If you laughed, so will others.

Going One-On-One: Building Relationships

The majority of mortgage origination sale is done through one-on-one contact during telephone calls, sales calls, and planned meetings. Our verbal communication skills are no less important during individual relations, but here, listening is of critical importance.

As a mortgage originator, listening is the tool with which you establish relationships, assess needs, and overcome objections. *If you discover that you've done most of the talking, you've blown it.*

Exhibit 3-2:   Interpersonal Sales Skills Pointers

1. It's key to realize that people are primarily interested in themselves and not you.

2. Take these four words out of your vocabulary—I, me, my, mine. Substitute for those four words three words—you, your and yours.

3. Make people feel important by listening to them, applauding and complementing them, refraining from arguing, and handling fighters properly.

4. Listen to people by looking at the person talking, leaning toward the speaker and listening intently, asking questions, and sticking to the speaker's subject without interrupting.

5. Finally, find out what they're after and what they like so you can tell them what they want to hear. Show them how they can get what they want.

Recognizing personality types (yours and those of the people you are trying to sell) is useful for building sales relationships. Adjust your approach, whether handling a fighter by avoiding conflict or trying to avoid idle conversation with someone rambling about facts, figures, and other business topics.

Asking questions is a first step to listening. Questions prompt people to talk so you can listen and establish a relationship. We introduced this topic in our needs analysis. Don't ask canned sales questions at the beginning of a conversation or before you've established a relationship. Yes, ask for the business. But don't ask for a loan two seconds after you introduce yourself to someone.

Ask questions using the "You" word, and stay away from mortgage banking:

Where are you from?
How long have you worked in this office?
What do you think of the way our football team is playing?

Are those your children in the picture?
Do you think Congress will pass the housing legislation?
Do you think rates are headed downward?

Ask their opinion. The highest form of flattery is to be asked for your opinion on something. For example, you are a new originator in a territory. You meet with a Sales Manager and ask, "Everyone tells me that you've been in this area for a long time and have been very successful. I would like your opinion on something. What do you think it takes for an originator to break into this market and become a force?" The manager will tell you what he or she expects you to do. If you heed their advice, they will have an interest in proving you right.

Establish a common ground. "Are those your children in the picture? How old are they? They're very pretty. I also have a seven-year old daughter." There are dozens of ways to establish common ground: family, religious or ethnic background, where you went to school, where you are from, former employers and sports. From there, you have something to talk about and the agent will see you as more than a salesperson.

As you enter the conversations you start by asking questions, find openings to interject sales topics. For example, the agent in conversation says, "I haven't been able to spend time working with legitimate buyers because my inventory of listings isn't selling and I'm constantly holding open houses." Your reply: "Is there anything I can do to help you move the listings? We do an excellent open house spread sheet. Would you like to see it?"

When directing a sales conversation, ask questions for which Yes is the only appropriate answer. "Would a program that qualifies your buyers for 20 percent more house and carries with it the safety of a fixed rate interest you?"

Body language is important for conversation and relationship building. It's one thing to ask the right questions of the right personality types. It's another to have the recipient of these questions believe that we are truly interested in anything but a sale.

1. Look at the person you're talking to. Make eye contact without staring them down.

2. Interject with nods of affirmation, or say, "I know what you mean."

3. Smile.

4. Lean forward and touch the person, but don't overdo it.

Telephone Sales

Telephone sales is an important and overlooked component of selling, and requires excellent verbal communication skills. When you take a rate inquiry call, you often have only one shot at selling that caller. Often you won't know the person on the line. It could be a Realtor or customer. It could be someone knowledgeable or someone who has little knowledge of real estate finance.

Debra Jones in the *Mortgage Generator Newsletter* notes that 50 percent of originators don't get the caller's name, only 25 percent get a telephone number, and even less find out what prompted the caller to call that originator's company. Each call is an opportunity to land a loan, but usually has one of two results:

• A 15-second answer to the rate question.

• A 30-minute conversation in which the originator attempts to educate the caller on the world of real estate finance.

In his sales seminar, Jack Davis relates a story of turning rate calls over to non-mortgage people who didn't have rates and were trained only in obtaining information. These people increased sales dramatically.

Why won't originators do the same? Usually they're busy doing something besides answering rate calls. They're tired of hearing from rate shoppers, and it's telling.

How do you turn a telephone inquiry into a sales appointment and a sale? Once again, by asking questions. Establish needs, find common ground, and do all the things you do in face-to-face sales.

The Sales Meeting

Most originators target real estate offices. The sales meeting is the one day each week that most of the Realtors are together so you can address them at once. Therefore, your number one goal—breaking into an office—should be getting invited to a sales meeting.

How do you go about getting an invitation? In the majority of offices, the manager controls the sales meeting agenda, so you must sell the sales manager "one-on-one" first. A few ideas:

- Send a letter before you visit. This establishes your professionalism and may "warm up" a cold call.

- Make an appointment. There may be 10 to 40 originators visiting the office. If you show respect for the manager's time, you'll get a better reception.

- Invite the sales manager to lunch, or find out what he or she likes to eat and bring in lunch, impromptu. They have to eat, so your meeting won't cost them time. If you take them out of the office for lunch, you'll eliminate distractions and provide a more open, neutral atmosphere.

- Have something to give out at the sales meeting that the manager will consider worthwhile. For example, a finance manual, FHA fact sheet, or new homes guide.

- Have a dynamite program to introduce to the agents. This can't be a program everyone else in town is pushing. It's either a program no one else has or one that agents must be educated about before using. Examples include:

  —Cap programs
  —Growing Equity Mortgages
  —Buydowns

- Provide a presentation on an educational topic you can deliver in 10 to 30 minutes.

Exhibit 3-3:   Short Sales Meeting Topics

- Introduce yourself and your company.
- Explain buydowns, growing equity mortgages.
- Sell a service:
    - —quick approval program
    - —open house spread sheets
    - —status reports
    - —pre-approval program
- Sell a program:
    - —cap program
    - —long term locks
    - —balloon
- Seminars and training available.
- Regulatory and legislative update.
- Dealing with bad credit.
- Alternatives for cash-poor homebuyers.
- Secondary market update.
- When can you use gifts?
- Condominium financing.

Doing a good job at a sales meeting is important for two reasons. First, you achieve our own goals (selling yourself, the company, or a product). Second, you endear yourself to the sales manager. One of the manager's jobs is to present a sales meeting agenda. You're part of that agenda. If you give a strong presentation, the sales manager shares in your success.

Goals to achieve during a sales meeting include:

- Introducing yourself and your background (briefly).

- Introducing your company. How large is it? What are its strongest features? What's its history?

- Introducing and selling a product. Sell the agents on a unique program or product benefits.

- Getting a seminar. When someone asks a question, say, "If this topic interests you, I can teach a seminar for the office." Schedule it on the spot.

- Getting leads on loans. There are many opportunities to land a loan during a presentation. Ask pointed questions. For example:

You're making a presentation on buydowns. You explain that 2.75 percent of the loan amount up front can achieve a buydown that increases qualification power by 20 percent. Give an example:

"To illustrate how this works, is anyone working with a buyer who desires a house up to 20 percent above the amount for which you have prequalified him or her?"

Perhaps you're not invited to a sales meeting. Does that mean you should stay in the office? Definitely not! The time just before or after a sales meeting is fruitful because most agents are in the office. Try bringing refreshments for the sales meeting, unannounced. Find out what the sales manager typically brings so you don't duplicate. You never know—you may get an invitation to speak, on the spot. Be prepared!

The Seminar

Make your seminars flexible as regards time. If you identify several distinct topics in your program, you can shorten or lengthen your presentation as required without sacrificing completeness or continuity.

For longer seminars, make sure there are adequate breaks, at least every 45 minutes.

Figure 3-4:   Landing a Loan at a Presentation

"This concludes my presentation on my company. Any questions?"

A. "Yes. How is your company working with marginal applicants who are short of cash?"

"Is this a hypothetical situation, or do you have someone you're working with right now?"

"I'm working with someone."

"What's the price range?"

"$100,000."

"There are many opportunities to limit cash investment in that price range. Would you like to get together after the meeting to go over these alternatives?"

B. "It's hard to envision how a 72-hour approval program would work for FHA, especially since you say that your average approval time is running 30 to 45 days. The only way to show you is to demonstrate a case. Is anyone working with an FHA purchase now?"

It's a good idea to provide refreshments, but keep the food light. You don't want them falling asleep!

Always allow time for questions. These are your opportunities to analyze the audience, and to open opportunities to further your goals.

Ask questions to encourage audience participation. Don't overdo it, but it's important for the target to participate to keep their attention. Make sure the questions aren't so simple you insult your audience, but aren't so complex they can't respond.

Periodically pause, analyze, and ask questions to make sure everyone is following you.

Don't overload the presentation. Keep to a few major points between breaks. Illustrate with examples, stories, and visual aids.

The longer the seminar, the more important it is that you're organized. Provide introductions and conclusions for major parts of the seminar.

Remember your goals, from obtaining creditability to securing business.

Exhibit 3-5:   Broker Presentation Checklist

Office:_____

Broker:_____

Date:_____

1. How long will I speak?
2. What information do I want to give them? What sales material loan programs, outlines, etc., will I need to distribute?
3. What are the learning objectives for the meeting?
4. What do I want them to do after I leave?
5. What can I do to prepare for the dynamics of listening? What will I do in my sales presentation to get them to listen?
6. How can I get them involved in an exercise they will feel good about?
7. How many senses will I appeal to?
8. How will I determine whether or not I have met my objectives?
9. How will I make my presentation different from other loan officers'?
10. What particular information regarding my topic does the broker want me to stress?
11. Is my presentation designed to be a "Win-Win" program?

Exhibit 3-6:   Questions Realtors Ask at Presentations

1. What do you think rates are going to do?
2. Does your mortgage company ask for conditions right before settlement?
3. How long is approval taking?
4. Do you portfolio loans?
5. Are you a mortgage company or a broker?
6. How do we know you (or your company) will be there?
7. What makes you and your company so special?
8. I don't like ARMs. Why should I recommend one?
9. Who do I call when there is a problem?

For example, question 2: "Does your mortgage company ask for conditions right before settlement?"

Sample answer: "I take it that you have had this problem come up before? Have most of you had that problem? What kind of conditions were asked for? Do you feel that these conditions could have been gotten up front?

"I'm glad you asked the question. I know now that we'll enjoy working together. I am not saying that I won't miss things in the process or that I don't make mistakes. I do know that the secret to hassle-free approvals is a complete loan application. It's my job to present a complete loan application and to do that the borrower must be prepared. Since you're concerned about a clean approval, I know you'll help me in my quest to make approvals happen.

"I have here pre-application kits that improve the application process 95 percent. I believe that 99 percent of underwriting conditions can be obtained up front."

Exhibit 3-7: Presentation Goals

1. To introduce yourself and your company to Realtors.
2. To introduce a product.
3. To gain credibility in your knowledge and expertise.
4. To gain another presentation—a seminar.
5. To gain prequalifications.
6. To obtain leads on new loans.
7. To pinpoint open houses to provide open house spread sheets.
8. To schedule a lunch with a particular type of Realtor.
9. To sell Realtors on a particular program or service.
10. To gain a commitment for future business.
11. To share your goals with the Realtors.
12. To find out who is transacting what type of business.

After setting objectives, organize the presentation to reach those goals. Your presentation should have this flow:

1. *Introduction.* Tell the audience what the presentation is about and why it's important. Pique interest.

2. *Body.* Give the presentation. It's important not to overload the speech. Deliver one important point every 5 to 15 minutes. The audience can retain no more than that.

3. *Conclusion.* Summarize what you said. Most important, remind the audience of at least one point you presented that made the presentation worthwhile for them. Key in on your goal.

Sample Summary of Significant Points of a Presentation

"Let me conclude my remarks on secondary marketing for Realtors by recapping the major points. First, the market is of extreme importance in our life. It can mean the difference between a good and dismal year. Second, there is no way to predict the future of interest rates. They are no more predictable than the stock market. Third, if you lock or float, you always have a 1/3 chance that you will be wrong. There is a 33 percent chance rates will go up, go down, or stay the same. Last, with such a strong possibility of being wrong, we wouldn't ordinarily play the game. So why should we in mortgage banking? Our cap program will enable your homebuyers to have the protection of a lock, with the possibility of going down when the rates go down. It's a win-win situation."

Exhibit 3-8:   Personality Types

Diverse—Results-oriented, success oriented. Don't waste time—time is money. Less interested in details as opposed to the big picture.

Analyticals—Organized. Want to know facts, figures, and other details. Know what is going on around the office. Absorbing, not necessarily talking.

Amiables—Open, conflict avoiders. Very helpful to those they like. Will not open up to everyone, however.

Expressives—Open and talkative. Will talk to the point of costing time, but can be very useful information sources.

Exhibit 3-9: Telephone Sales Conversation Example

Caller: "What are your points for conventional 9 1/2 percent mortgages?"

Originator: "Are you purchasing a new home?"

Caller: "Yes, we just put a sales contract in this morning."

Originator: "Did you work through a real estate agent?"

Caller: "It was a for sale by owner."

Originator: "Are you also selling your home that way?"

Caller: "No, we're renting now."

Originator: "Is it your first home?"

Caller: "Yes."

Originator: "Congratulations. What is the sales price and loan amount?"

Caller: "Sales price is $100,000 and loan amount is $95,000."

Originator: "Is there any particular reason why you're not going with FHA financing?"

Caller: "I think we make too much money."

Originator: "There are no income limits for FHA financing and you could save several thousand dollars with cash up front. When is your settlement date?"

Caller: "In 30 days."

Originator: (rise in excitement) "You really have to get moving! I would be happy to meet with you and explain the advantages of FHA as well as several alternatives such as buydowns which start at a much lower rate than 9 1/2 percent, and growing equity mortgages which pay off in 15 years. Are you free tonight after work or tomorrow morning?"

Caller: "Tonight would be fine."

Exhibit 3-10: Questions to Ask a Telephone Rate Shopper (A-Z)

a. What's your name?

b. Are you working with a real estate agent?

c. Who is it and what office is he or she from?

e. How did you hear of our company?

f. What is your telephone number?

g. Would you like me to work up some numbers and call you back?

h. Is it a purchase or a refinance?

i. How long have you owned the home?

j. What is the rate and mortgage type of your present mortgage?

k. What's your reason for refinancing (lower rate or cash out)?

l. Have you ever refinanced before?

m. Do we hold your present mortgage?

n. What's your settlement date?

o. How many points is the seller paying?

p. What's the sales price?

q. What's the loan amount?

r. Is the sale contract contingent upon selling your present home?

s. Is this your first home purchase?

t. Are you familiar with adjustable rate mortgages, buydowns, FHA, and growing equity mortgages?

u. Do you intend to lock your loan in or float the rate?

v. Has an originator qualified you?

w. Has someone gone over the list of items you'll need to get together to make a loan application?

x. How long do you expect to be in the house?

y. How much do you expect your income to increase in the next five years?

z. What tax bracket are you in?

Exhibit 3-11: Telephone Skills

To better serve you, I need more information:

1. Is this a single-family home?_____

2. Is it owner-occupied?_____

3. Is it a refinance or a purchase?_____

4. Refi: Who presently has the loan?_____

5. Purchase: Have you signed a contract?_____

6. Name and address of the real estate agent you are doing business with:

Name:_____

Address:_____

_____

Telephone #:_____

Give your name again and ask their name.

7. Caller information:

Name:_____

Address:_____

_____

Telephone #:_____

I can close the loan. What this means to you is that you get the house you desire to purchase.

Exhibit 3-12: Telephone Use Checklist

1. When I close a call do I ask for an appointment?
2. Do I communicate to the caller the benefits of meeting with me to discuss his or her needs?
3. Do I sound friendly and relaxed?
4. Do I have an objective for making the call?
5. Do I keep my objective in mind or do I get sidetracked?
6. Do I smile when talking?
7. Do I really listen to what the caller is saying? Do I really hear him or her?
8. When I'm interrupted by a telephone call, do I act and sound perturbed?
9. Do I use memory joggers?
10. Do I interrupt the speaker?
11. Do I answer the caller's questions by seeking additional information about his or her request?
12. Am I so brief that I will be considered rude?
13. Am I too talkative and take too much time?
14. Do I gain control by asking open-ended and closed questions?
15. Do I listen more than I talk?
16. Do I sound canned or is my conversation spontaneous?
17. When answering my telephone do I say, for example, "This is John Smith speaking, how may I help you?" rather than just hello?
18. Have I ever asked someone in the office to listen to my calls and give me constructive criticism?
19. Have I ever tried using a tape recorder beside me while I make calls so I can hear how I sound?
20. Do I follow the 3-2-1 formula using my caller's name three times, please twice, and thank-you once?
22. Do I maintain control and interview the caller or does the caller interview me?

Education as a Selling Tool

An important ingredient of sales is service. So far, we have defined service in terms of closing deals as quickly as possible, without problems. By doing so, you're providing service where it's most important—the Realtor's bank account. Realtors lose their commissions if deals fail to close, and lose opportunities to create other deals if you waste their time with problems.

Instead of simply expediting deal closings, what if you actually helped Realtors sell homes? Providing referrals is one way to help Realtors sell. You can also help turn potential purchasers into homeowners by providing financial analyses of programs and tax deductions, or providing a financial breakdown of programs available for listings.

Providing education to Realtors and others is truly "value added" service. Realtors graduate from licensing and post-licensing classes with only a rudimentary introduction to the world of financing. They know that a broad understanding of programs and packages will help them sell houses. You have a unique opportunity to garner new Realtors' loyalty on day one of their career by doing the following.

Providing Basic Finance Training

Again, the right time for you to create a working relationship is the first day of a Realtor's career. It's not surprising that Realtors give their business to people who help make sense of the most confusing aspect of their new profession. There are many opportunities to teach basic finance to new Realtors:

- *At the licensing level.* For states with licensing requirements for Realtors, you can lecture for a community college, private school, or even a licensing school run by a real estate company.

- *Post-licensing classes.* Many major real estate companies have post-licensing courses on a range of topics, including finance. Their training departments commonly invite originators to teach finance classes.

- *On-the-job training.* Conduct individualized sessions with Realtors. Realtors might never have the opportunity to absorb basic finance unless you give them one-on-one tutoring as a follow-up to their licensing sessions. If an office has several new agents, hold small group sessions.

Keep such training sessions general and brief. In-depth sessions confuse novices. Generally, you should cover loan sources (FHA/VA/conventional), qualification, down payments, and forms of mortgage insurance. Don't get involved with secondary financing and discussions about seller concessions, but do provide some material on these subjects for your students to read once they are comfortable with the basic material.

Teaching Seminars through Continuing Education

Many states with licensing provisions for Realtors also require them to complete continuing education classes. Here, you're guaranteed an audience of experienced Realtors, as they must have sufficient credits to keep their licenses current. You may teach continuing education classes in finance through colleges, private schools, real estate company training departments, or even through your own mortgage company.

Even when states have no continuing education requirement for Realtors, you can present a series of advanced courses designed to help agents understand financial products and how to use these products to sell houses. Emphasize finance as a selling tool rather than just something Realtors must deal with to complete a transaction.

Topics you may present include sessions on financing sources such as FHA or VA, or product types such as adjustable rate mortgages and buydowns. Your subjects may even be a bit arcane, on more specific topics such as condominiums and the self-employed applicant. The key is to find a timely topic, one of interest to the target group.

Sponsoring Realtor Seminars

An alternative to teaching finance seminars yourself is sponsoring them. Arrange to have an expert speak on real estate sales. However, flying in experts can be expensive and, since you aren't doing the actual training, the bond created may not be as tight as it would be if you were the featured guest. An alternative is to find an expert already on travel and offer to defer expenses for a planned seminar. Even so, the cost for sponsoring seminars yourself may be prohibitive.

Holding Homebuyer Seminars

Team up with a Realtor to hold a seminar for potential home purchasers. You may provide the seminar and flyers while the Realtor provides the location and advertising. Financial planners, CPAs, and settlement attorneys might also present portions of the seminar. Such participants are a source of referrals for you.

Seminar Hints

Introductions

Establish rapport and a positive first impression on participants before your seminar. The ideal time to begin is at the door, greeting your guests. You will find that both you and the participants are more at ease if you have the opportunity to meet them beforehand, rather than being the "Mystery Speaker."

Capture your audience's attention from the very beginning of your seminar:

- Have a well-known local Realtor or special attendee introduce you.
- Tell people about yourself. Keep it brief and be a bit humble.

- Humor is great when it's been tested.
- Introduce special guests.
- Smile, be sincere, and look your guests in the eye.

Exhibit 3-13: Instructor's Role

It's your responsibility as the seminar instructor to serve as the organization's role model. The concepts and principals you present must emanate a professional, self-confident and knowledgeable representation of you and your mortgage company. Positive behavior and statements produce satisfying and successful seminars. The following tips should prove helpful in preparing a positive experience for you and your audience:

- Study, understand, and practice your presentation.
- Communicate clearly, both orally and in writing.
- Use a variety of methods, activities, and aids.
- Demonstrate enthusiasm, understanding, and a sincere interest in the attendees. Smile.
- Listen attentively and repeat questions.
- Remember, credibility is based upon your ability to adhere to your time schedule.
- Reinforce your effectiveness by checking the audience's level of understanding.

    —"Am I making myself clear?"

    —"Are these issues making sense?"

    —Ask for feedback.
- Tell the participants what they should expect from the class.
- Summarize the content covered in the session.
- Keep a positive attitude. Avoid being defensive.
- Remain in control of the session. Stay on track.
- Do not let the question and answer session drag on or fizzle out. Be sure to keep it within the time limits. When you are nearly out of time, tell your audience, "There is time for only one more question."

Exhibit 3-13   (Continued)

- Keep your answers brief and concise, but be sure to answer questions as completely as possible. A good format to follow is either a one sentence or yes/no answer.

- Always have a "power" statement, phrase, or story to close the session. You may review the key points covered.

Some Don'ts:

- Don't grade questions by telling one questioner, "That's a good question," but not telling others their questions are good, too. Just answer the question.

- Avoid answering questions with "Well, obviously" or "As I said in my talk." These are put-downs.

- Don't allow one person to ask all the questions. Simply say, "Many others have questions. I'll get back to you if there is time."

- Don't use negative body language. Don't put your hands on your hips while you are listening to the questions or answering, or fold your arms over your chest.

- Don't point one finger at your audience while you are speaking. That is a scolding pose and it makes you seem preachy.

- Avoid "off-the-record" statements.

- Never hedge or avoid answering a question. Give your audience a straight answer.

- Don't argue with the questioner. If he or she persists, offer to discuss the question with the person after the meeting.

- Don't sink to the level of a nasty questioner. Usually, the audience will take care of a rude member of the audience if you remain the "good guy."

Exhibit 3-14: Seminar Planner

Prior to the meeting

Publicity	*Agenda*	*Location/Equipment*
_____Invitations	_____Plan Agenda	_____Reservations
_____Registration	_____Preprint	_____Refreshments
_____Brochures		
_____New Releases		
_____Special Guests		

Day of the meeting

Location	*Equipment/Supplies*
_____Seating	_____Audio/Visual Set-up
_____Temperature	_____Handouts/Business Cards
_____Refreshments	_____Name Tags
	_____Microphones

The Meeting	*After the Meeting*
_____Greet Guests	_____Collect Extra Materials
_____Distribute Handout	_____Evaluate Session
_____Be Available at Breaks	_____Ask for Feedback
_____Get Business Cards	_____Follow-up with New Contacts

Exhibit 3-15: Effective Seating Arrangements

Here are some good arrangements for seminars.

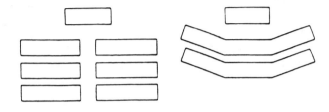

. . . .

These arrangements encourage good group interaction.

. . . .

And this arrangement facilitates small group-within-a-group interaction.

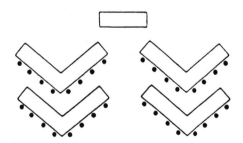

Exhibit 3-16: Planner Guide

Subject/Topic:_____

Intent:_____

_____

_____

_____

_____

Specific Points to Cover:_____

_____

_____

_____

_____

Handouts:_____

_____

_____

_____

_____

Visual Aids:_____

_____

_____

_____

The following exhibits are program guidelines for producing courses and seminars.

Exhibit 3-17: Basic Real Estate Finance

Course Description: A legislative update followed by a general comparison of FHA/VA/Conventional eligibility requirements, downpayments, loan limits, and insurance requirements. Ratio and residual methods of qualification are introduced in a case study.

I. Legislative Update:

    A. FHA

    B. VA

    C. FHLMC

    D. FNMA

II. Program Comparison:

    A. FHA

        1. Eligibility

        2. Maximum Loan/Downpayment

        3. Mortgage Insurance Premium

        4. Miscellaneous Facts

    B. VA

        1. Eligibility

        2. Maximum Loan/Downpayment

        3. Finding Fee

    C. Conventional

        1. Eligibility

        2. Conforming vs. Jumbo

        3. Private Mortgage Insurance

        4. Miscellaneous Facts

Exhibit 3-17   (Continued)

III. Qualification:

    A. Ratio Method

        1. Income

        2. PITI

        3. Debts

        4. Conventional/FHA/VA Ratios

    B. Residual Method

        1. Taxes

        2. Housing Costs

        3. Family Support

    C. Case Studies

Exhibit 3-18: Real Estate Finance Alternatives

Course Description: An introduction to the complex world of mortgage instruments. The program includes discussions on biweeklies, GEMs, GPMs, 20-year fixed rates, buydowns, adjustables, negative amortization, and a basic method for comparing the performance of different programs over time.

I.   Fixed Rate Products

    A. 30-Year Fixed

    B. 15-Year Fixed

    C. 20-Year Fixed

II. Fixed Rate Hybrids

    A. Balloons

    B. Buydowns

        1. Calculation

        2. Lender Subsidized

        3. Compressed

    C. Growing Equity Mortgages

    D. Biweekly Mortgages

III. Adjustable Rate Mortgages

    A. Components

        1. Margin and Index

        2. Caps

        3. Adjustment Term

    B. Features

        1. Negative Amortization

        2. Conversion

Exhibit 3-18   (Continued)

IV. Comparisons
   A. Worst Case and Other Scenarios
   B. Loan Comparison Chart

Exhibit 3-19: Unique Purchasers and Challenging Situations

Course Description: How to turn a challenge into a sale. Non-resident aliens, condos, investors, self-employed applicants, bad credit, no cash, co-borrowers, and gifts.

I. Eligibility Issues
   A. Purchaser
   B. Property
   C. Mortgage Insurance

II. Income
   A. Stability
   B. Increasing Income
   C. Lowering PITI

III. Credit
   A. Poor Credit History
   B. Lowering Debts

IV. Cash
   A. Seller Pays Closing Costs
   B. Gifts
   C. Low Down Payment Programs
   D. Borrowing
   E. Selling An Asset

Exhibit 3-20: II Seminar Checklist

For:_____Real Estate Company

On:_____ 19_____

Planning:

_____   Time allocated:_____

_____   Location:_____

_____   Number of people:_____

_____   Experience level: from_____ to_____ (_____average).

_____   Knowledge of seminar subject:
                                from_____ to_____ (_____average).

_____   Subject requested: FHA Qualifying____Blue Book____

                Max Mtg____Conv. Qualifying____Underwriting____

                FHA Programs____Conv. Programs____

                Special Programs____ Other_____

_____   Seminar format: Classroom____Workshop____

                Small Group____Sales Meeting____Other_____

_____   Ask broker to have agents bring calculator: yes____no____

_____   Any other speakers: yes____no____

_____   Will I speak before____or after____meeting?

_____   Is there a caravan after? yes____no____

_____   Available props board:_____

Exhibit 3-20   (Continued)

overhead projector_____VCR_____other_____

_____ Food: yes_____no_____before_____

during_____after_____

_____ Other:_____

Preparation:

_____ Prepare outline of seminar subject

_____ Practice presentation of seminar subject

_____ Prepare seminar materials

_____ Seminar pads

_____ Make, stamp, and highlight point sheets

_____ Business cards

_____ Other supplies: price line stickers_____

amortization cards_____consumer brochures_____

note pads_____items needed at application_____

flyers_____

_____ Order food

_____ Pick up food

_____ Purchase glasses, napkins, etc.

_____ Other:_____

Exhibit 3-20   (Continued)

Presentation:

_____   Arrive 15-30 minutes early

_____   Arrange materials

_____   Give it my all

_____   Write down unanswered questions

_____   Leave remaining food (and materials, if appropriate)

_____   Other:_____

Follow up:

_____   Call with answers to questions

_____   Send thank-you note

_____   Double visibility for next 6 to 8 weeks

_____   Call company with all rate changes on seminar subject
                     (3 to 4 weeks)

_____   Highlight seminar subject program on point sheets
                     (3 to 4 weeks)

_____   Set appointment with the "slower learners" to explain
                     seminar subject one-on-one

_____   Other:_____

Exhibit 3-21: Homebuyers Finance Seminar Materials

Table of Contents

4

Targeting Your Market

After learning your role as a loan originator and achieving a broad knowledge of your role in the mortgage industry, you must identify the market and the needs of target groups within that market before you start selling. How? As the first step in your professional or consultative sales approach, you must first conduct a *market needs analysis*. To understand the needs of your market, you must first identify the targets within that market.

The Realtor

Realtors control 80 percent of the home purchase sector of the origination market. A cross section of Realtors reveals subgroups within that segment:

- Sales managers.
- Top producers.
- New agents.
- Part-time agents.
- Sales personnel for builders.

Each subgroup requires a tailored sales approach. You might approach a sales manager to schedule a sales meeting appearance. New agents are prime targets for training classes. You might reach part-time agents through mailings rather than office visits. Top producers require more intense targeting efforts such as lunches and other individual meetings.

Builders

The new home sector of the real estate profession represents a significant portion of the origination market, and, again, requires a different sales approach. Originators may sell long-term "bulk" commitments or pursue individual or "spot" builder business. The originator might target real estate sales personnel employed by or working with the builder, or approach the builder and/or developer directly to establish a relationship.

The Homebuyer

The entry of corporate giants into the mortgage field (Citicorp, Prudential, Sears, Ford Motor, and General Motors) has increased direct consumer contact, especially during periods of heavy refinance volume. Direct home buyer contact would typically be accomplished through company-sponsored mass media efforts—direct mail, newspaper ads, and radio or television spots. However, it's possible for the originator to accomplish direct contact individually through local ads, flyers, or direct mail. The originator might work with a Realtor to sponsor a first-time homebuyers' seminar. Presentations and other targeted sales efforts may also focus on present homeowners in a position to refinance, potential first-time homebuyers, or those in the process of "moving up."

Service Providers

It stands to reason that those who provide services to homebuyers would make excellent networking references for you. This method to reach the greatest concentration of potential customers is second best only to working through Realtors. The following are agents who provide services vital to real estate transactions:

- Settlement agents.
- Insurance agents.
- Pest control companies.
- Appraisers.
- Radon testing firms.

Other professionals who come in contact with potential homebuyers or refinance candidates include financial planners, CPAs, banks, and credit unions. Many small financial institutions prefer to refer mortgage business. Even a mortgage company with a limited product menu might refer business to other mortgage companies. For example, a second trust originator might refer first trust clients to another lender, and vice-versa. A savings and loan that dosen't offer VA loans might refer such business as a service to its customers.

Needs Analysis

After you are aware of your basic target groups, you must perform a needs analysis to determine the appropriate sales approach and product concentration. How do you determine these needs? By asking questions.

- In what price range does the Realtor specialize?
- Does the Realtor have foreign clients?
- What is the average down payment on transactions?
- How mobile are the customers?
- Are they first-time homebuyers, or "move-ups?"
- What is the average length of time between contract and settlement?
- How long does the homebuyer/owner intend to stay in the house?

- What is the potential for income growth?
- How many points do the sellers typically pay?

The possibilities are endless. Yet, the more information you gather, the more effective your sales and marketing plan will be. An effective information-gathering and planning stage eliminates objections before they appear. The close can be confirmed before the presentation is through. Consider the following exhibit, where we list specific marketing and needs analyses for the Realtor sub-group.

Exhibit 4-1: Realtor Subgroup Needs Analysis Questions

a. How many agents does the office employ?

b. What is the ratio of full-timers to part-timers?

c. Who are the top five selling agents?

d. On the average, how many transactions per month does the office complete?

e. What is the average sales price and price range of these transactions?

f. What is the ratio of new to experienced agents?

g. What finance training is presently provided the agents? By whom?

h. When does the office hold sales meetings?

i. What are the office hours?

j. What mortgage products does the office emphasize? Fixed rate, ARMs, or buydowns?

k. What loan types does the office emphasize? FHA, VA, conforming, or jumbo?

l. What mortgage company does the office use most often?

m. Who are the loan officers for these companies?

n. Why does the office use these companies?

o. What problems has the office had with mortgage companies in the past?

p. Is the office affiliated with a mortgage company?

q. What is the most important factor in loan placement?

- quick approval?
- established relationship with the originator?
- easy qualifying program?
- low rate?
- low points?

r. What is the ratio of the new home transactions to resale transactions?

s. On average, how many open houses does the office hold each week?

Exhibit 4-1   (Continued)

    t.   Does the office have any agents who sit on new homes projects?

    u.   What is the best way to distribute rate sheets and flyers?

    v.   What days of the week is it important to have rates available?

    w. Does the office prefer to receive written or verbal loan statuses?

    x.   What is the present source of finance news for the office?

    y.   What direct consumer contact programs does the office undertake?

    z.   What would the office like to know about me or my mortgage company?

Exhibit 4-2: Steps to Complete the Market Survey and Determine Our Niche

Determine the:

1. Number of real estate firms and the number of Realtors for each area.
2. Population of the area.
3. Industries in the area.
4. Median income level.
5. Turnover or transience in the area.
6. Population increase or decrease in the area, and the reasons for it.
7. Sales through real estate community.
8. Products being offered in the area.
9. Market share of companies, i.e., competitors and real estate firms.
10. Number of sales and in what price ranges.
11. Loan-to-value ratios for these sales, and the average LTV.
12. Location of competitors.
13. Names of top producer Realtors.
14. Real estate companies in the area.
15. Different types of financing available.
16. Number of new construction loans vs. those for existing homes.
17. Types of buyers in each area.
18. Competition's advantages.
19. Competition's operational advantages and weaknesses.
20. Depreciation rates in each area.
21. Industry shut-downs or changes in any industry in our market.
22. Competitor currently servicing the market and their methods of marketing.

Exhibit 4-2   (Contined)

23. Percentage of Realtors who use computers.

24. Competitor's ratio of volume to the number of originators in each office.

25. Experience level of Realtor base. Are they veterans or trainees?

26. Alternative sources of volume other than Realtor and builders.

27. Competitive advantages and disadvantages of your branch office, using the branch office self-assessment form at the end of the following market survey section.

Determine Your Niche

The market survey is divided into three areas:

1. The demographics of the community.
2. The real estate and Realtor market survey.
3. The competition for financing.

The purpose of the market survey is to determine your market niche in your area. A self-assessment of your office based on results of the survey will follow. We must determine how we are or are not capitalizing on this market niche, differentiating ourselves from the competition, and maximizing the bottom line.

I.   Demographics of the community

1. Total population_____. Number of counties this includes_____.

2. Describe the fluctuations in population (percentage increase or decrease) and explain what changes are responsible.

    _____

    _____

    _____

3. Please list the percentage before each category in describing the types of buyers in your market.

    _____% Conventional
    _____% Low income ($30K and less)
    _____% Middle income ($40K to $60K)
    _____% Upper-middle income ($60K to $100K)
    _____% Upper-upper income ($100K plus)
    _____% Government

4. What is the median income level of the population in your area? $_____

5. Is this a transient community? Yes_____No_____
The average homeowner stays in their home in this area approximately _____ year(s).

6. Divide the number of sales made in your area over the last 12 months into the following price ranges. (List percentage for each.)

   1.____$30,000 to $50,000   3.____$ 75,000 to $100,000
   2.____$50,000 to $75,000   4.____$100,000 to _____

7. What is the average loan-to-value in your market? The average LTV for each price range above:

   1._____2._____3._____4._____

8. What is the percentage of permanent sales for:

   new construction_____ existing homes_____

9. What is the depreciation rate in your market (e.g., of the homes sold, what is the percentage that fall out or go into foreclosure?)? The depreciation rate:_____

10. What major changes have occurred with large industry employers in your area that will affect or have affected the real estate industry (i.e., shut downs, mergers, leveraged buy-outs)?

   _____

   _____

   _____

   _____

   _____

II.   The real estate and Realtor market survey

1.   Rank in order the name of the top 15 real estate firms in
     your area and the number of Realtors in each based on
     dollar volume [i.e., Merrill Lynch, 50 (20). NOTE: If there
     are several offices run by the same company, list the
     number of offices in parentheses].

1._____	6._____	11._____
2._____	7._____	12._____
3._____	8._____	13._____
4._____	9._____	14._____
5._____	10._____	15._____

2.   Please list the top real estate producers (top 20%) of the
     above 15 offices and the names of the Realtors in those
     firms.

Co._____	Co._____	Co._____
1._____	1._____	1._____
2._____	2._____	2._____
3._____	3._____	3._____
4._____	4._____	4._____
5._____	5._____	5._____

3.   What percentage of all homes in your area were bought
     and sold through a real estate firm?

_____

4.   What is the percentage breakdown of homes sold by the
     real estate firms listed in question 1 (e.g., what is their
     market share)?

1._____	6._____	11._____
2._____	7._____	12._____
3._____	8._____	13._____
4._____	9._____	14._____
5._____	10._____	15._____

5. List the number of real estate firms that use a computer to pull up rates rather than relying on the relationships with area loan officers.

1._____4._____7._____
2._____5._____8._____
3._____6._____9._____

6. In your market area, what is the average number of years of experience of the Realtor base (e.g., number of veterans vs. number of trainees)?

_____

III. The Competition for financing

1. Who are your top five competitors and why?

1._____Why?_____
2._____Why?_____
3._____Why?_____
4._____Why?_____
5._____Why?_____

2. What products are being offered in your market that you compete with most (e.g., your products in comparison to other similar products. Please be specific—list all features)?

1._____
_____
2._____
_____
3._____
_____

3. What competitors have the highest percentage of your financing market and what is the percentage?

1._____ 4._____
2._____ 5._____
3._____ 6._____

4. Where are your competitors' headquarters and/or service operations that service your market located?

1._____
2._____
3._____
4._____
5._____

5. How does the competition differ from your company? (List advantages and disadvantages.)

_____

_____

_____

_____

_____

6. What operational advantages or disadvantages exist with your competition (i.e., turnaround time)?

_____

_____

_____

_____

7. Who is currently servicing the market and what are their methods of marketing?

_____

_____

_____

_____

8. Of your top five competitors, what is the ratio between the number of loan officers with each office and the volume the office generates per month (i.e., every loan officer = $1,500,000 production)?

1._____

2._____

3._____

4._____

5._____

9. What are the best selling products in your area and why? (List benefits and features.)

1._____

2._____

3._____

4._____

5._____

10. List several alternative sources of volume other than Realtors and builders.

1._____

2._____

3._____

4._____

5._____

IV.   The branch office self-assessment

Now that you've completed your market survey, our objective is to enhance volume, better our service and better the
competition.

1. Determine and describe your market niche.

    _____

    _____

    _____

    _____

2. How do you plan to target this market?

    _____

    _____

    _____

    _____

3. How does this plan differ from what the competition is
    doing?

    _____

    _____

    _____

    _____

4. List five steps of action you plan to take within the next
    month to meet this market niche.

    1._____

    2._____

    3._____

    4._____

    5._____

Exhibit 4-3:   Critical Needs Analysis

Agent:_____
Date:_____

Transition phrase: To ensure that I give you the best service possible, it's important that I ask you a few questions.

1. How long have you been in the real estate business and how do you like it? _____

2. What is the territory that you cover? _____

3. Are you a lister or a seller? _____
   Lister: Qualify property._____
   Seller: Qualify purchasers._____

4. What percentage of your business is:
   Residential_____
   Commercial_____
   New Financing_____
   Assumption_____
   Other_____

5. What percentage of new financing is:
   Government (FHA/VA) _____
   Conventional_____
   Jumbo_____

6. What loan programs do you feel most comfortable with?
   Fixed Rates   [ ]
   Buydowns   [ ]
   ARMs   [ ]

7. What loan programs do you want to know more about?_____
   _____

8. What lenders are you using and what do they do to earn your business?_____

9. What would you like to see from a lender that you are not seeing now? _____

10. If you could identify the single biggest problem you are having in our real estate business today, what would it be?_____

Exhibit 4-3   (Continued)

11. If I help you solve that problem would you give me the opportunity to do business with you? _____

12. Would you prefer your office or mine for applications? _____

Referral phrase: Do you know of anyone else who can use my services?

Exhibit 4-4:   Questionnaire for Targeted Real Estate Office

Real estate office: _____

Number of agents: _____

Monthly average of total volume of new loan sales: _____

Names of top 25 percent agents: _____

The percentage of sales that are:
    new loans _____

    government loans _____

    conforming loans _____

    jumbo loans _____

    insured loans _____

Who are the top three mortgage companies currently being used, and why?

Do sellers generally pay discount, origination, and closing fees? _____
_____

What do they pay? _____

Is there a weekly sales meeting? If so, what day and time is it held? ____
_____

Do the broker, owner, and manager allow mortgage companies to provide training seminars at the sales meeting? If so, how can I give one?
_____

Do the agents handle their paperwork, or do secretaries? How about the top agents? _____

How can I get loans from this office? _____

Exhibit 4-5: The Originator Monthly Marketing Plan Calendar

Sunday	Monday	Tuesday	Wednesday	Thursday	Friday	Saturday
	1 OFFICES AB (GEM program) LUNCH – KEY AGENT 5 key letters	**2** OFFICES B SALES MEETING (GEM program) MAILING LIST 5 key letters	**3** OFFICES A MAILING – REAL ESTATE 5 Key Letters	**4** OFFICES B STAFF MEETING STATUS SPREAD SHEETS 5 Key Letters	**5** OFFICES A (rates/status) 5 Key Letters	**6** OFFICES B (rates/status)
7 Open Houses Subdivision	**8** OFFICES A (newsletter) LUNCH – KEY AGENT 5 Key Letter	**9** OFFICES B (newsletter) SALES MEETING 5 Key Letter	**10** OFFICES A SEMINAR (GEM program) MAILING – SETTLE AGENTS 5 Key Letter	**11** OFFICES B STAFF MEETING STATUS SPREAD SHEETS 5 Key Letter	**12** OFFICES A (rates/status) OFFICES C 5 Key Letter	**13** OFFICES B (rates/status)
14 OFF 5 Key Letter	**15** OFFICES B (GEM program) COLD CALL 5 Key Letter	**16** OFFICES A SALES MEETING (GEM program) 5 Key Letter	**17** OFFICES B MAILING – FINAN. PLANNERS 5 Key Letter	**18** OFFICES A STAFF MEETING STATUS SPREAD SHEETS 5 Key Letter	**19** OFFICES B (rates/status) 5 Key Letter	**20** OFFICES A (rates/status)
21 Open Houses Subdivision 5 Key Letter	**22** OFFICES B (newsletter) LUNCH – KEY AGENT 5 Key Letter	**23** OFFICES A SALES MEETING (newsletter) 5 Key Letter	**24** OFFICES B SEMINAR (GEM program) MAILING – INDIV. 5 Key Letter	**25** OFFICES A STAFF MEETING STATUS SPREAD SHEETS (GEM program) 5 Key Letter	**26** OFFICES B (rates/status) OFFICES C 5 Key Letter	**27** OFFICES A (rates/status)
28 OFF	**29** OFFICES A COLD CALL 5 Key Letter	**30** OFFICES B SALES MEETING 5 Key Letter	**31** OFFICES A 5 Key Letter	*Offices visits assume one appointment per day *Key letters assume 5 calls following up (as well as reference call) *GEM is program marketed for month		

Targeting Realtors

This section is devoted to the "bread and butter" of the majority of the mortgage industry—the Realtor. As the mortgage industry has changed in the past few years, so has the real estate industry and its relationship with mortgage bankers. Many more real estate companies own mortgage companies (or vice-versa), or have clearly established relationships with one lender. Others limit access to the offices to two to four lenders, and still others conduct in-depth interviews with originators who wish to solicit a particular real estate office.

The Territory: Key Accounts List

Typically, mortgage originators are assigned a geographic area. The following are advantages and disadvantages of geographic territories.

Advantages:

- The proximity of offices lessens travel time.

- There is a greater chance that the listing agent or selling agent referred will be in an office you service.

- You can become expert in the type of business indigenous to your particular area. For example, it may be an FHA area due to the price of the average unit sold.

Disadvantages:

- If the area supports only one type of business, you may not become familiar with all mortgage products.

- There may be little opportunity to diversify, particularly when one market slows down (for example, a high priced area).

Other than geographically, how are territories developed? An originator might be assigned offices of particular real estate companies. This is almost always true of real estate owned mortgage companies. You might also be assigned particular builders or new subdivisions. What makes sense?

Diversification is always important. It's nice to have offices close together, but map out territories that include differing economic strata, even if you split some towns.

If you are a spot originator, you should visit some projects to capture spot builder business, sell commitments, or make sure the builder is familiar with you and your company when your agent sells a new home and requests that you take the loan application. There are times when resale business is slow and new homes sales are still strong, or vice-versa. Diversification is as important to an originator as it is to a corporation.

The key accounts concept plays an important role in territory development. Offices and Realtors will hold different weights in your marketing plan. A Realtor becomes a key agent by referring business to you on a regular basis. There may be twenty offices in your territory, but only seven offices of those on the key accounts list. In those seven offices, there may be only thirty-five agents out of two hundred that are key agents. Also, there may be key agents in non-key offices.

Key offices and key agents are your targets. The other offices might be on a general mailing list. Include on your list one office that you are breaking into to offset the chance of a key office lessening in importance. Send key agents individual letters, take them to lunch, and call them regularly.

One last issue to consider when selecting territories and key targets—what about key agents outside your territory? You may have a friend in an "outside" real estate office, or perhaps a loyal agent has moved to a real estate office on the other side of the city. Should you continue to serve that agent? What if the agent is in a territory or office serviced by a peer?

There's no easy answer to this question. The Realtor should have some input concerning this issue. If the Realtor insists on a continued relationship with the original loan officer and pledges a significant portion of business, it's difficult to deny his or her wishes.

The Offices and the Office Route

Real estate offices make up the significant portion of a spot originator's territory. As we identified the key accounts concept, it's logical to identify key offices and derive a route by which you visit them.

The tendency will be to arrange office visits geographically—that is, to visit offices near each other during the same trip. This may not be a good idea if the offices vary in business activity and hours. Exhibit 4-6 is a sample office visit schedule for 10 offices located in two main areas. Note that there is some variation of sales call hours and office combinations.

Exhibit 4-6: Weekly Office Visit Schedule

Mon.	Tue.	Wed.	Thur.	Fri.	Sat.	Sun.
10: Off. 1	10: Off. 4	10: Off. 7	1: Off. 4	11: Off. 1	10: Off. 9	1: Builder
11: Off. 2	11: Off. 5	11: Off. 8	2: Off. 5	12: Off. 2	11: Off. 10	2: Builder
12: Off. 3	12: Off. 6	1: Off. 1	3: Off. 6	1: Off. 3	12: Off. 6	
3: Off. 7	1: Off. 9	2: Off. 2	4: Off. 9	3: Off. 4		
4: Off. 8	2: Off. 10	3: Off. 3	5: Off: 10	5: Off. 5		

Offices will vary in composition and as regards business activity. Here are a few variations:

- Some offices are large offices with constant activity, day after day.

- Others are smaller with part-time agents and have activity during the evening hours.

- Some offices will specialize in listing activity, others in sales.

- Some offices will sell a large proportion of new homes.

The Office Visit. As much as we've described Realtor relationships, mailings and meetings, nothing happens until you visit the office. "Calling on offices" is a major part of any originator's marketing plan. We've identified two particular problem areas with originators' calling routines:

1. There's a tendency to visit offices solely to deliver rate sheets. You should have an objective each time you call on an office. You should analyze each visit immediately afterward, and develop a plan to follow up.

2. There's a tendency to stay in your office or anywhere but the Realtor's office. Jim Pratt calls this "call reluctance." Call reluctance isn't unique to the mortgage industry—in most industries salespeople give up before making enough calls to be effective. Pratt likens call reluctance to stage fright. This correlation is even more apparent in our last real estate topic.

The Dreaded Cold Call. Walking into an office for the first time ranks with the fear of public speaking as far as the originator is concerned. How can you make the cold call more palatable?

First, by mailing letters, newsletters, rate sheets, and introductory packages to the Realtors and the sales manager for a few weeks before your first visit. When you show up (especially with a name tag), they will recognize you.

Make an appointment to meet with the manager, secretary or an agent outside the office before or during your first visit. This will bring more direction to the visit and provide an "in."

As tough as it is to do, you should make cold calls constantly. Once you break into a territory and close loans, it's too easy to stay in the mortgage office and babysit loans in process.

When you finally go out, there's a tendency to gravitate toward established offices. Yet, territories should be fluid. At any given time, an office is becoming less important due to lack of business or some other reason.

To counterbalance this effect, you *must* cold call offices. Without consistent, forward sales efforts your techniques will dull or even disappear. While mailings and status reports throughout your territory keep receptions warmer, there's no substitute for face-to-face sales efforts directed at an office or key agent.

"The Key Players

The key players in a real estate office are the manager, duty agent, secretary, and top producers. We will address each individually because each plays an important role in mortgage origination.

The Manager. We've already introduced the manager and his or her importance in the development of the sales meeting agenda. The manager is important for several other reasons:

1.   The manager sets policies for your access to the real estate office and for the distribution of rate sheets. The manager may decree that you (and other originators) aren't allowed beyond the front desk, or put the Realtor's desk area off limits. Then you're stuck dropping rate sheets in the mail room.

2.   Many times the manager is responsible for meeting the continuing education needs of the agents, or supplementing company-sponsored training. The manager must approve or set up training seminars.

3.   The manager places many loans, especially for part-time and new agents. He or she may begin a relationship for you by matching you with an agent with a particular need.

The Duty Agent. Most real estate companies have an agent that sits at the front desk to handle walk-ins or call-ins. This agent is a duty agent or floor agent. In offices that try to keep originators from the agent desk area, getting past the duty agent is your immediate goal.

Larger offices may have full-time receptionists to handle guard duty up front. Whether the guard is a floor agent or a receptionist, they're still guards.

In an issue of the *Mortgage Generator*, Debra Jones addresses the topic of dealing with a guard. Some tactics: calling on the receptionist and developing a relationship, having an appointment with a particular agent (always a good idea), or having something to drop off on a particular agent's desk.

Because duty agents take call-ins and walk-ins, it's usually a good idea to spend some time with that person. He or she is a barometer of office activity, may know who is working on contracts, and may have had call-ins who need prequalification. It never hurts to ask for the business.

The Secretary. The secretary may or may not be the same receptionist we spoke of as the full-time guard. Regardless, the secretary of any office is of prime importance, not only for access, but as the "information center" of the office.

Make a sales call directed toward the secretary—take him or her out to lunch, and make sure he or she gets whatever you're giving the agents. There's much the receptionist can tell you about the agents: who does the business, who's new in the office, who gets along with whom, what the rules are, and what the manager likes and dislikes.

The secretary typically handles the contract paperwork for the offices (depositing checks and sending the contract to the corporate office). This means that the secretary can become a valuable source of information regarding new business. Further, the secretary typically keeps a logbook or bulletin board with listings and sales for the month.

The Top Producer. One of your goals is to service the top producers in your territory. By definition, top producers are difficult targets because they're busier, have out-of-the-way offices (they may occupy private offices or the corner of a real estate office—look for the plaques), are being pursued by many other originators, and already have relationships established to handle their heavy volume of business. A difficult target calls for a more concentrated approach: personal letters, lunches, and appointments.

Is this worth the extra effort? The adage, "10 percent of the sales people do 90 percent of the business," is especially true in the real estate industry. The industry is full of part-timers and non-productive individuals. Top agents really do dominate the business.

Exhibit 4-7: Call Critique

_____   _____
          Client   Date

Instructions: Complete immediately after a call. Keep with customer profiles for review prior to next call on this client.

	Yes	No
Did I make a professional impression?	_____	_____
Did I talk too much?	_____	_____
Was I an effective listener?	_____	_____
Did I pick up the personality styles?	_____	_____
Was my interview/presentation tailored?	_____	_____
Did I find the needs?	_____	_____
Did I cover the features/benefits?	_____	_____
Did I address objections properly?	_____	_____
Did I get a commitment?	_____	_____
Did I close effectively?	_____	_____
Did I plan for the next action?	_____	_____
Overall, was the call effective?	_____	_____
Have I made at least 5 good calls here?	_____	_____
Would I do business with me?	_____	_____

What could I have done differently?

_____

_____

What will I do differently next time?

_____

_____

_____

Exhibit 4-8: Office Visits

Objectives:

1. To obtain a meeting with the sales manager or a key agent.
2. To set up a seminar or a sales meeting.
3. To prequalify an applicant.
4. To obtain lists of open houses to provide spread sheets.
5. To discover what contracts have been written by whom and what deals are in the works.
6. To introduce yourself and your company to the sales manager or key agent.
7. To deliver:
   Rate Sheets
   Program Flyers
   Open House Spread Sheets
   Status Reports
   Newsletters
   Prequalification Letter
8. To ask for the business and get a loan application.
9. To take a loan application.
10. To introduce a program.
11. To learn office rules such as rate sheet delivery policies.
12. To meet the receptionist or secretary.

Realtor call sheet for the week ending wed., _____/_____/_____

Please indicate "P" for phone call, "V" For office visit

Realtor Number	Mon.	Tues.	Wed.	Thur.	Fri.	Sat.	Comments

Loan Officer Initials_____Page_____of_____

**Exhibit 4-9:   What is Your Commitment to
                  Your Customer Base?**

- To provide you, as a Realtor, with financial training.

- To keep you informed of changes to requirements affecting the processing and closing of mortgage loans.

- To be available to answer your financing and qualifying questions.

- To assist you in choosing the most appropriate financing options for your customers.

- To explain our programs to you and your customers at loan application, and to answer any questions either of you may have.

- To return all phone calls promptly.

- To always be honest, open, and above-board with you and your customers.

- To assure you of the most accurate, efficient service possible.

- To ask for your comments and suggestions on how to improve our service.

- To make the entire mortgage loan process as easy and pleasant as possible for both you and your customers.

Exhibit 4-10: Thank-you Letter

Dear Realtor

As Branch Manager, I would like to thank you for the mortgage application recently made by your client. Please remember that I am available to assist you in any way possible.

Your client's application will be personally processed by one of our mortgage processors. I have enclosed a business card so you may contact the processor if you have any questions.

We will be keeping you up-to-date throughout the loan process with our weekly loan process report (from application to commitment) and the loan progress report-committed loan (from commitment to closing). These reports will list conditions that still need to be satisfied to complete the mortgage process.

Remember, we value your business and thank you again for choosing ABC Mortgage.

Cordially,

Branch Manager

Exhibit 4-11: "Preferred Realtor" Letter

Dear Preferred Realtor:

ABC Mortgage is testing a special program for selected Preferred Brokers. This program, designed especially for the real estate professional, will feature:

- Expert Processing
- Faster Service
- Common Sense Underwriting
- Dependable Status Reports

This special program will be available for the next 120 days on single family primary residences. As an inducement to try it, we will refund the $300.00 application fee to your client at closing. We will also pay for the appraisal and credit investigation.

At the end of the trial period, we will invite you to meet with the people who made the program a success to discuss additional ways to make this service better for you.

We at ABC feel that you owe it to yourself and your clients to try this innovative program, not once but many times during the trial period.

Sincerely,

Dave Hershman
Loan Originations Manager

To get started, call today 444-4444, ext. 444 (Preferred Broker Desk), and ask for your special code number.

Exhibit 4-12: Sales—Ten Dos & Ten Don'ts

James L. Hennessy, Jr. and James C. Pratt

Mortgage Banking Magazine, May 1987

The first quarter's end of any new year is time for a change. Winter has wound down, spring is here, the boys of summer are sharpening up their cleats, and every living human being has broken one or more new year's resolutions. Resolutions, like rules, are made to be broken. We know that some will endure while most will not, and that is all part of the game we play with ourselves. Rather like natural selection, most of us believe that our strongest resolutions will survive and become part of our lives. Significantly, the "strongest" and the "most important" are not necessarily the same.

Salespeople are highly competitive, so it is normal and positive for them to aspire to high achievement; it is also normal for them to expect that hard work will make it happen. It is common, however, for them to overlook the steps that will lead there. And those steps are nothing more than the ordinary things salespeople must do everyday.

The routine, the mundane. That is where the change must start if a selling career is to be revitalized and kicked into high gear. Offered here are some things to think about, a place to start. First, some things to stop doing, and them some things to start doing. Let them help reinforce those rapidly fading New Year's resolutions.

Ten Things To Stop Doing

Stop talking so much on calls—Most salespeople love to talk, and calls provide them with a stage, an audience and a role to play. Try listening more, especially if you are there to fact-find. When you talk too much, you are sacrificing control of the situation. The listener has the power in almost any conversation simply because he/she can ask questions and guide the speaker.

Use good questioning and listening techniques to learn more about your prospect, uncovering needs, concerns, and feelings that your competition missed by talking too much. As a rule of thumb, if you are talking more than 40 percent of the time on a call, you are blowing it.

Exhibit 4-12   (Continued)

Stop giving up after the second call—Just about every one who sells has heard of the 80/20 rule, but no one seems either to know why it is so consistently true or who noticed it first. The rule states that 80 percent of our business comes from 20 percent of our customers. Another aspect of the rule is that 80 percent of the business is done by 20 percent of the people.

To test the rule, try a quick experiment: take the number of loans you have originated in the last three months, multiply times 80, then determine how many offices those loans came from. Now, of the offices you call on, what percentage do these most active clients represent? Probably around 20 percent, if the rule holds.

Interesting you say, but of what significance? Studies show that:

- Almost half of all salespeople make one call and quit . . .
- One quarter of all salespeople make two calls and give up . . .
- But 80 percent of the sales come after the fifth call.

Therefore, if the rule holds true (as it has for generations), it means that *only 20 percent of the salespeople make more than five calls on a prospect.*

Think how powerful that knowledge is, and how you can use it. If you can make at least five *effective* calls, you can outpace 80 percent of your competitors. Notice that the word effective is emphasized. Merely dropping off rate sheets and making other "show 'n go" calls don't count.

Salespeople are highly competitive, so it's normal and positive for them to aspire to high achievement; it's also normal for them to expect that hard work will make it happen.

Charles De Montesquieu could have been talking about this phenomenon 250 years ago when he observed, "Success generally depends on knowing how long it takes to succeed." If he was right about that, if you just have to know there is light at the end of the tunnel, can you think of a single reason not to give your prospects more than five solid calls?

Stop "dropping in" on important clients—Use appointments whenever possible, particularly if you are targeting the boss. Appointments virtually guarantee you a hearing, as well as enhanced prestige and professionalism in the eyes of the client.

Exhibit 4-12   (Continued)

Have you ever called on an office and run into several of our competitors hanging around, hoping for a moment of the decision-maker's time? If you had arranged an appointment, which of the group is the boss most compelled to see?

While it's true that appointments are often unnecessary, it's as true that those who work by appointment whenever possible occupy a higher rung on the client's ladder. And doubly so if the client is a time-conscious, performance-oriented, "driver" type of individual.

Stop worrying about the quantity of your calls—Worry more about their quality. Many Realtors have taken steps to limit the activities of lender representatives who they feel waste their people's time—gated barricades are an example. They believe that loan officers who do little more than drop off business cards and rate sheets are doing just that: wasting time.

The mortgage representatives who get the attention of brokers and agents alike are the ones with something to say when they call. These reps are viewed differently because they are purposeful in their approach to the job. They aren't content to do the "hi-how-ayas" and disappear until next week, but rather will find ways to make their calls meaningful.

Professionals like these will do twice the business of the others—with half the calls.

Stop ignoring your professional image—The same professionals mentioned previously realize that they must be conscious of the impression they make on others. They may not like the uniform of business any more than those among the competition who insist on making a statement of flamboyant individualism by their dress. But the pros realize something very important: right or wrong, people are judged by the impressions they make. And you never get a second chance to make a first impression.

How would you feel about a lawyer who arrived in court to argue your case dressed for the golf course? Or a heart surgeon who showed up to perform your operation looking like a refugee from "Dance Fever"? You would probably doubt their seriousness, if not their competence.

Exhibit 4-12   (Continued)

It's no different in the mortgage banking industry. Realtors need to have confidence that the lender they recommend is competent, efficient and professional. After all, Realtors work with their buyers and sellers very closely—sometimes they become part of the family.

Even though there is a school of thought among loan originators who believe that eccentricity equals uniqueness equals more business, it flies in the face of reality. In the real world, why would anyone who is really serious about their business seek to be disadvantaged right off the bat?

Stop throwing away your opportunities to think—Most salespeople do three things right after a call. They buckle up, start the car and turn on the radio. The first two are fine, but there's a major alternative to the third—thinking.

Thinking time is precious and rare, far more so than the weekly top 40. There's only a little time during a busy day to devote to thinking. Many of those who deny themselves opportunities for thought during the day find themselves doing it at night—late at night—when they are trying to get to sleep.

If you must listen to something between calls or if you face rush hour traffic gridlock on a regular basis, consider an alternative to "the hits"—perhaps some of the many motivational and instructional cassette tapes that are available.

Stop making commitments you can't keep—It's one of the easiest things in the world to make promises, and one of the hardest things to keep them. Some salespeople believe you should promise whatever it takes to get in the door, and worry about details later. Wrong. Your clients are neither stupid nor short of memory.

When it comes to a transaction Realtors have been nursemaiding during a period of months, they will remember when a loan agent fails on his or her promise to fund the loan by a specific date, or promise that the rate is locked in. Likewise, they will recall exaggerated claims on other matters as well, and they will not forget a busted deal, a lost commission or a dissatisfied buyer.

Exhibit 4-12   (Continued)

Stop making only "comfort" calls—Comfort calls serve a wonderful purpose, but many loan officers spend far too much time on them, especially when a case of call reluctance flairs up. Everyone who makes calls for a living suffers from call reluctance from time to time. It's that feeling when you just cannot bear to put on your professional smile and go boldly into the lion's den again.

Suddenly things like picking up your dry cleaning, getting the car washed, or buying new brake linings become extremely urgent. Indeed, one feels that movie matinees were created for salespeople with call reluctance.

Even those things, however, are preferable to getting in the habit of calling on clients who don't do any business, but make you feel welcome and secure. The same is true if you find yourself concentrating on a particularly friendly (but low-producing) agent in an office filled with surly high achievers.

The pros know that comfort calls have a constructive purpose, that they can help combat call reluctance. They call on the easy ones first thing in the morning. The resulting glow of acceptance hardens into a suit of armor for the rest of the day, one that will blunt the claws of even the fiercest lion in the jungle.

Stop letting your professionalism slip—In addition to several of the items discussed previously, there are many more ways to let down your professional guard. Talking down the competition for example. Nobody likes to hear it, and derogatory comments reflect far more on the speaker than the accused. If you harbor any doubt about that statement, look no further than any political campaign you care to name and the ads it produced.

Along the same lines, don't shade your remarks too much in your favor. Unless you are a complete actor, it comes across phony and contrived. Speak to your personal and corporate strengths, not the other fellow's weaknesses.

At industry meetings, do you wind up with other loan agents, swapping war stories and playing "can-you-top-this?"? If you do, your action is being beaten by the pros who are circulating and meeting clients.

Exhibit 4-12   (Continued)

Another one of the easiest things in the world for salespeople to do is to assign blame when a deal goes sour. The processors, the funders, the underwriters, the escrow company and attorneys are all at fault. If not them, then the buyers, the sellers, or the agents are at the root of the problem.

The smart pro writes it off and learns from a bad situation, instead of grousing to anyone who will listen about who was at fault. Recriminations don't do anything except stick in people's minds, especially if they are valid.

Stop thinking that your education is over—Salespeople have large egos, especially if they've been successful. After all, they are usually making more money than most of the organization, and there are a few pats on the back outside the company.

The real pros know ego is a defense mechanism that has an important place in the complex componentry of motivation. They also know there's great truth in the maxim "He who stops getting better, ceases being good."

Continuing education has a place in everyone's life, and that education can be in non-industry related areas, limited only by one's interest and imagination. Using motivational cassette tapes, taking night classes once a week, and devoting a specific number of hours a week to reading instead of watching television are all methods of continuing education.

Why is continuing education critical for a salesperson? Simply because a sales person's job is nothing more than dealing with people—different types of people. Learning more about how to converse with them, what turns them off, and what turns them on is all part of making the process work to your advantage.

Ten Things To Start Doing

Make sure each of your calls has a purpose—Many of your clients are installing various sorts of barricades to help them regulate lenders' reps and other callers. If you have ever wondered why they go to the trouble, your answer may be as close as your next call. Look to see if your competitors are purposeful or just wasting everyone's time. Chances are good that most of them tend to loll about in idle conversation. They lack purpose in their calls—they are not there for a particular reason.

Exhibit 4-12   (Continued)

You can avoid falling into this very common trap by being aware that every call must have a purpose other than idle conversation. If there is not an immediately obvious one, it is up to you to create one. It can be a program/rate change, rumbles in the secondary market or in local real estate. There is always something to take with you to give your call purpose and meaning. It is up to you to find it.

Start analyzing your calls—the best time to do it is immediately after you leave the office. It is too easy to turn on the radio and deny yourself the chance to think. Jot down several things you did right, then jot down several things you did wrong. Also, make certain you understand the next step with the client, and jot it down too. When you seize your opportunities to be constantly learning, constantly improving, you become aware of something very interesting. You become aware that each call can be your best call, and that future ones can be better still.

Start analyzing your clients' performance—You cannot afford to spend your valuable time with clients who do not produce for you. An office that used to be a big one for you may have lost a key agent, surrendered market share to another firm or otherwise may have become a lower priority. Be sure to recognize when this happens and adjust your efforts accordingly. You can only afford to "carry" a small number of low performers. Ask yourself some thorough questions about your client base every 90 days, such as:

- On a scale from 1 to 10, how has this office performed?
- Do they get their share of buyers, or mostly listings?
- How many lenders do they deal with?
- Do I get my fair share of their business?
- How many calls have I made on them in the last 90 days?
- Is my best agent there one of their high performers?

According to the 80/20 rule, you should turn over a fairly high percentage of your clients annually, 20 percent of them are probably doing 80 percent of your business.

Exhibit 4-12   (Continued)

Become a student of people—People are the artist's palette and canvas of the professional salesperson. Just as an artist needs to understand the full potential of the range of colors, so must a salesperson know how to deal with the differences in people. Most realize that people are different and must be approached differently. Many, however, do not realize that there are clues in observable behavior that can help them anticipate how others will react to certain situations. And that can be of inestimable value to a salesperson. There are numerous books available in libraries on the subject of social style analysis, and it is the paramount concept in *Selling Skills for Mortgage Loan Professionals* by James L. Hennessy, Jr.

Get organized—Time is a salesperson's most valuable tool. Using it to the maximum advantage is often the sales person's greatest challenge. Salespeople tend to be ebullient, vivacious creatures for whom detail is a despised implement of torture. It takes discipline and perseverance to master time and make it work for you. Disciplined pros make and follow a flexible work schedule to maximize their selling time. In our business, it generally consists of office time planned at the beginning and end of the week, beginning and end of the day, with selling time in between. Of course you must be in the office to interact with the support staff, but it is not the place to spend your bread and butter hours. It is just so easy to get sucked into tasks and phone calls that are better performed at a different time of day. Do these things as bookends to your selling day— early or late.

Learn to prioritize your time and tasks. It is fundamental to any time management program, and there are a number of effective ways to accomplish it. Regardless of whether you use a day, week, or month-at-a-glance-type system, or content yourself with a "things to do today" pad, the important thing is to use it.

Add the personal touch—You are the difference between your company and the rest of the field. Use that individuality to do the little things that will make you stand out from the crowd. Personal notes to clients to thank them for their time or to follow up an appointment are an example. They need not be lengthy or complex, just literate and sincere. Along the same lines, leave a brief note on your business card when you miss key contacts in offices during the day. Hardly anyone else does that, and it means your card will get noticed among the multitude. It is a people business, and creativity really counts. Find ways to make your personality come through in your approach to the business.

Exhibit 4-12   (Continued)

Create a notebook for presentations and objections—A presentation notebook will help you utilize your thoughts before going into a presentation, and provide reminders for key points that will work with your client's social style. An objections notebook helps you handle the hurdles every salesperson encounters along the path to getting a commitment. The amazing thing is that there really are no more than 8 or 10 objections out there. True, they may come in slightly different forms from time to time, but there are basically less than a dozen typical objections that even the unseasoned loan officer can cite. Notebooks like these are easy to start and maintain; you are required only to write down an objection when you hear it the first time, or jot in a presentation idea when it occurs to you. They are powerful and effective refreshers, regardless of your experience level.

Always conduct an interview before making a presentation—This is the most fundamental rule in selling, as any sales trainer will tell you. It is also the most frequently broken, even by the most seasoned professionals. You have to know what the needs are before you can do an effective job of meeting them. If it is as simple a concept as it sounds, why then do most salespeople opt to "shotgun" every feature, benefit, aspect and permutation of their product line? Is it not far easier to ask a few questions and then target shoot? It is, if one can but listen rather than talk.

When you find yourself tempted to rattle off the same list of programs that every other loan originator recites to the client, do yourself a favor—stop. Then take out something to write on and say the magic words, "Do you mind if I ask a few questions?" The next sound you will hear is yourself in the act of leaving 80 percent of your competitors behind. You are in the process of joining the elite 20 percent who do most of the business when you discover the power of effective questioning and fact-finding. After you bring some of the client's concerns and interests out in the open, you can go about preparing a powerful and beneficial presentation. Most interviews are very casual, conversational in nature, rather than formal sit-across-the-table affairs. Whether formal or informal, it is all the same—the discovery of needs and opportunities to be of service. That is what selling really is.

Exhibit 4-12   (Continued)

Update your understandings before starting a presentation—You have done your fact-finding, clarified your understandings of the client's needs and prepared your presentation. You are all set, right? Well, almost. Before you launch into your presentation, it is very wise to go over your understandings once more with the client—they may have changed. Suddenly, your inspired solution to a client concern is not relevant any longer because the situation is different from your last meeting. Prior to starting, just ask if you can restate your perceptions of things quickly to make sure nothing has changed. If every thing is the same, you have refreshed the client's memory. If some things have changed, you will not waste the client's time on those items, or perhaps you may have bought yourself a little time to think of something else during the call for the new situation.

Become a student of your industry—The best way to truly understand how to get business is to understand how your clients do business. Think like your customers, and you will seldom be short of ideas on how to serve them better. If you are to think like them, you must know the business inside and out, in some ways even better than they know it themselves. And that kind of knowledge does not come easily. Take real estate courses. Many states are requiring lenders' representatives to become licensed anyway, and more are likely to follow suit. Look for other courses to take, seminars to attend as well. Pick an agent you know well and spend a day with her/him. Keep an agent company at an open house and pick his/her brain. Most importantly, use an ancient secret of wisdom: sit at the feet of the masters. Find one or more successful professionals and spend time with them to learn about your field, your role, and ultimately, yourself. All of these dos and don'ts reflect changes in everyday routine. It will not do much good if you treat them like most resolutions of this time of year. Give them a thorough evaluation and implement the ones you believe can be helpful in revitalizing your career and recharging your batteries. In the final analysis, that implementation, that conscious decision to act and effect change, is the most important resolution of all.

What is Customer Service?

We've already established that the key to success in origination is customer service. Therefore, to determine how we approach the marketing effort, we must clearly set the boundaries of customer service. It's through this service that we satisfy the needs of our targets.

target group ⟶ needs ⟶ service ⟶ sale

What is customer service? It's much more than providing rates and program descriptions to our market. Customer service entails the following factors.

Availability

Realtors want originators to be available 24 hours a day. After all, the real estate business is not a nine-to-five affair. Gone are the days when bankers sat in their offices waiting for customers to walk in and apply for loans. What must you be available for?

- To prequalify customers before the agent takes them "house hunting."
- To provide rate and program information, especially near the time that the contract is to be presented.
- To take the loan application.

You will perform many of these functions after hours. Even during office hours, you may be out of the office when the Realtor calls to schedule an appointment or ask a question. Therefore, there must be ways for the Realtors to reach you after hours or while you're on the road. Tools of accessibility include a:

- Numeric pager which displays the caller's phone number.
- Voice mail or message system.
- Car phone or portable phone.
- Message system for the car phone.

- Home telephone answering machine.

The electronic age has reached the mortgage industry. It may not be necessary to use all of these devices, but every originator must, at minimum, have in place a paging or home message system of some description.

Availability goes beyond electronic gimmickry. It's impossible for a salesperson to be available 24 hours a day, 365 days a year. There are vacations, weekends off, or merely times when the originator is in meetings or taking loan applications and must not be interrupted.

- If you will be absent from the office, you must secure another originator to cover new business calls and instruct your processor to handle status calls. You should contact Realtors with contracts "in the works" to inform them of your absence and of the backup system in place. If your absence is to last several days, you should write every Realtor or target with whom you do business.

- If there is a regularly scheduled meeting through which you can't be disturbed, for example, a Thursday morning sales meeting, you should inform Realtors to call at other hours. Realtors have meetings, too—they will understand and work around the schedule. Education is the key.

- If the meeting is unscheduled or you are in loan application, you must leave specific information with the person answering the phones. It's better to hear, "Kevin is in loan application and will be available after 4:00 pm" than, "Kevin is on the road." The second reply is unprofessional and the Realtor will wonder why you are failing to return calls from "the road."

Follow-up

Once you take the loan application, your job really begins. You must follow up diligently throughout processing, underwriting, and closing processes:

- Let the Realtor know how the application went (if the Realtor wasn't present), and if there are possible qualification or processing problems.

- Introduce yourself to the listing agent and transmit the above information.

- Conduct weekly status sessions with Processing to ensure that all information is being received on time and as stated at loan application. Inform the Realtor if there is a problem with the applicant's follow-up information.

- Secure any "significant conditions" the underwriter requests. Significant conditions are non-standard conditions that Processing does not ordinarily procure.

- Make sure the Settlement department is prepared to get the settlement instructions and closing documents out on time.

- Call applicants and Realtors after settlement to make sure that closing went smoothly.

"Value Added" Service

Availability and follow-up are expected of you. If you want to become a top producer, you must go a step further by providing "value added" services. What are "value added" services?

- Status reports. Providing weekly status reports to the Realtor is a step beyond normal follow-up. While status reports are a means of follow-up, they are also a sales tool. You can advertise that you provide weekly status reports on rate sheets and flyers. Further, delivering the status report is a legitimate reason for you to make an office visit. Providing reports to a listing agent moves you one step towards establishing a working relationship. The following exhibits are sample status reports.

Exhibit 4-13: Loan Progress Report Pending Loan

Applicant:	Joe Sample	Date:	June 9, 1989
	165 Main Street	Appl. #:	ROC8900001
	Rochester, NY 15676		
Company Name and Address:	ABC Realty		
	15 South Street		
	Rochester, NY 14565		
Sales Associate:	Morey Sales		
Mortgage Consultant:	Miss Sibley		

- -

THE FOLLOWING ITEMS HAVE NOT BEEN RECEIVED

- -

Item	*Date Requested*
Return Application	6/05/89
Appraisal	6/05/89
Credit Report	6/05/89
VOE—Kodak	6/05/89
VOD—Investors Mutual Fund	6/05/89
Loan Rating—Security Pacific	6/05/89
Loan Disclosure	6/05/89
Recent Pay Stub—Kodak	6/02/89
All Parties Agreement—2nd Req.	6/08/89

Exhibit 4-14: Committed Loan Report

Applicant:	Joe Sample	Date:	June 9, 1989
		Property:	2-5 Main Street
			Rochester, NY 14555
Realtor:	ABC Realty	Appl. #:	ROC89000343
	15 South Street		
	Rochester, NY 14565		
Attn:	Morey Sales		

Dear Morey Sales:

We can all experience "Shared Success . . . The Sibley Way" by working together to close your customer's loan. To expedite the closing process, we wish to inform you that the following conditions still need to be satisfied:

1. At the time of closing, applicants sign original mortgage application.

2. Receipt of a Certificate of Occupancy dated no more than three months prior to closing.

3. Health Authority approval of septic system dated no more than three months prior to closing.

We would appreciate anything you could do to assist us in satisfying these conditions. As a reminder, the mortgage commitment will expire on July 18, 1989.

If you have any questions, please feel free to call our office.

Sincerely,

Sibley Corporation
Underwriting Department
2 State Street/Suite 600
Rochester, NY 14614
716-232-1190   1-800-742-5391

Exhibit 4-15: Status Form
American Residential Mortgage Corporation

DOCS EXPIRE
_____

**STATUS FROM
AMERICAN RESIDENTIAL
MORTGAGE CORPORATION**

ORIGINATOR _____

PROCESSOR _____

LOAN TYPE _____
SALES PRICE _____
APPRAISED VALUE _____
LOAN AMOUNT _____

SETTLEMENT ATTY.
_____
PH # _____
CONTACT _____

SELLING AGENT

LISTING AGENT

DATE APPROVED _____

EST. CLOSING DATE _____

PROPERTY ADDRESS

(H)　　(O)

(H)　　(O)

PURCHASER

RATE　　　PTS　　　EXP. DATE

	REQ	REC	2ND	REC	REMARKS	DISCLOSURES	REQ	REC	2ND	REC
APPLICATION						GOOD FAITH EST.				
CREDIT REPORT						TRUTH IN LENDING				
BUSINESS CREDIT REPORT						PROGRAM DISCL.				
APPRAISAL						MARYLAND DISCL.				
FINAL INSP.						LOCK-IN AGREE.				
SALES CONTRACT						GOOD THINGS				
LISTING						BUYDOWN TERMS				
ADDENDUM						72-HOUR				
PRE-SALE LETTER						PRE-APP. AUTH.				
EMPLOYMENT	REQ	REC	2ND	REC		CERT. AND AUTH.				
						OCCUPANCY DISCL.				

						FHA LOANS		REC	VHDA	REC
						PICTURE/SSID			LOCK-IN DISC.	
PREV EMPL.						HUD/ASSUMP DISCL			ACQUIS COST	
						LEAD PAINT DISCL			ECOA	
PAY STUB - 30 DAY						MIP DISCL			RESERVATION	
RETIRE/SS/DISAB						AMEND CLAUSE			BUYER AFF	
IND TAX RETURNS						REAL ESTATE CERT			SELLER AFF	
CORP TAX RETURNS						VA LOANS			RECAPTURE TAX	
W2s/1099						VA ASSUMP/LOCK DISCL			QUALITY CONTROL	
P&L/FINSTMT/PERJ						VA INDEBT			BD DISC PROVIDER	
RELO LETTER						FED COLL POLICY			BD DISC BORROWER	
ASSETS	REQ	REC	2ND	REC	REMARKS	VA DEBT QUESTION				
DEPOSIT						COE/VET STATUS				

						EXPLANATIONS	REQ	REC	2ND	REC
						CREDIT				
						INC IN ACCT				
APP/LOCK FEE REC			$	$ App	$ CR $ LF	NEW LN/ACCT				
3 MO STMTS						REFI LTR				
COPY CANC DEP CK						DEC LN AMT				
STOCK/BONDS/NOTE						JOB GAP/HIST				
GIFT LTR/DONOR VERIF										
DEPOSIT W/GIFT						SETTLEMENT REQ	REQ	REC	2ND	REC
EQUITY ADVANCE						HAZARD INSURANCE				
LIABILITIES	REQ	REC	2ND	REC	REMARKS	TERMITE REPORT				
MORT						SURVEY				
						TITLE BINDER				
						FINAL INSP				
						PMI CERT				
						CONDO DOCS				

						SUBMISSION	SUB	SUB	RESUB	APP
PMT HIST						IN HOUSE				
PERSONAL						TO INVESTOR				
						TO PMI CO				
						CONDITIONS				
AUTO										

ORIGINATOR NOTES ON CASE:

CHILD CARE					
DEED REL/PYOFF					
DIV DEC SEP AGR					
RENTAL					

RESIDENCE	REQ	REC	2ND	REC	REMARKS
SALES CONTRACT					
HUD 1					
LEASE					
LEASE					
DEED OF TRUST					
STATUS SENT					
DATES					

- Open house spread sheets. Any tool that helps the Realtor sell a house is "value added." The open house spread sheet provides information that helps an agent evaluate open house "walk-ins," and helps the potential buyer to evaluate the house. The examples of open house sheets on the following pages show homebuyers they can afford the house being in question. Basic qualifying information can convert weekend "browsers" into purchasers.

- Seminars. Seminars, from basic qualifying to advanced topics such as condominium financing, also help agents sell houses. Homebuyers' seminars put you in a position to "sell" potential homebuyers *for* the Realtor. You may conduct portions of each seminar on a one-on-one basis to sell individual homebuyers in such areas as leverage, real estate as an investment, or the tax advantages of home ownership.

- Information. Informational materials include finance manuals, newsletters, and bulletins. Developing a relationship in which the Realtor depends on you for information is, once again, going well beyond the minimums of availability and follow-up. This alters the Realtor's perception of you as just a salesperson to an expert in the field of finance. For your target market to consider you as such is a prime objective of any professional or consultative salesperson.

- Using service to get referrals. While referrals are an appropriate subject at every stage of the sales process, the law of reciprocity states that the pitch for referrals will be more effective if given when you perform a service rather than during a sales pitch. The following is a list of situations that are opportunities for "referral farming."

    After prequalifying a customer. When the Realtor says, "Thank you," it's time to say, "You're welcome. I'm glad to be of service. Is there anyone else in your office currently working with new clients whom I might also help?"

Exhibit 4-16

SUPERIOR SERVICE MORTGAGE
CORPORATION

Conventional Financing Alternatives
30 Year Loans

Property Address
123 MAIN STREET
ANYTOWN, USA

Presented by
YOUR REALTOR
REAL ESTATE OFFICE

Phone Numbers
(714) 123–4567

Listing Price
$200,000.00

10% Down			20% Down	
Loan Amount:	$180,000.00		Loan Amount:	$160,000.00
FIXED	ADJUSTABLE		FIXED	ADJUSTABLE
10.375%	7.950%	INTEREST RATE	10.375%	7.950%
1.50	1.50	POINTS	1.50	1.50
$20,000.00	$20,000.00	DOWN PAYMENT	$40,000.00	$40,000.00
2,700.00	2,700.00	POINTS ($)	2,400.00	2,400.00
1,500.00	1,500.00	CLOSING COSTS	1,500.00	1,500.00
1,040.67	1,040.67	IMPOUNDS	938.00	938.00
767.47	588.08	INTEREST (15 DAYS)	682.19	522.74
1,250.00	1,250.00	PROPERTY TAX (6 MOS)	1,250.00	1,250.00
420.00	420.00	FIRST YEAR INSURANCE	420.00	420.00
$27,678.13	$27,498.75	CASH TO CLOSE	$47,190.19	$47,030.74
$1,629.73	$1,314.51	PRIN. & INT.	$1,448.65	$1,168.45
208.33	208.33	PROP. TAXES	208.33	208.33
30.00	30.00	HAZARD INS.	30.00	30.00
66.00	66.00	P.M.I. **	58.67	58.67
$1,934.07	$1,618.84	TOTAL MON. PAYMENT	$1,745.65	$1,465.45

** PRIVATE MORTGAGE INSURANCE

The closing costs and impounds are estimates.
The impounds and the monthly payments for property taxes,
hazard insurance, and PMI are optional on the 20% down programs.

Contact John Terveer for further financing information.

313 N. SECOND AVE. * SUITE J * UPLAND, CA 91786
(714)981–1400

Exhibit 4-17

SUPERIOR SERVICE MORTGAGE
CORPORATION

Conventional Qualifying Worksheet
30 Year Fixed

07/10/90

BORROWER:	JOHN SMITH
ADDRESS:	123 MAIN STREET
CITY:	ANYTOWN, USA
PHONE – D.:	(714) 123–4567
N.:	(714) 987–6543

REALTOR:	ANY REALTOR	RES.:	(714) 123–4567
OFFICE:	ANY OFFICE	BUS.:	(714) 987–6543

SALES PRICE:	$200,000.00		LTV
LOAN AMOUNT:	$160,000.00		80.00%
INTEREST RATE:	10.375%		

DOWN PAYMENT   **$40,000.00**

CLOSING COSTS:

POINTS	1.50	$2,400.00
APPRAISAL		250.00
CREDIT REPORT		50.00
LOAN PROCESSING FEE		250.00
DOC PREP FEE		100.00
TAX SERVICE		60.00
ESCROW FEE		480.00
TITLE INSURANCE		215.00
RECORDING FEE		30.00
TOTAL COSTS		3,835.00

IMPOUNDS:

PROPERTY TAXES (6 MONTHS)	$1,250.00	
INSURANCE (FIRST YEAR PREMIUM)	420.00	
PREPAID INTEREST	682.19	
TOTAL IMPOUNDS		2,352.19

CASH REQUIRED TO CLOSE   **$46,187.19**

INCOME	$5,400.00	NECESSARY RATIOS: 28 / 36
INCOME	0.00	
OTHER	0.00	TOTAL MONTHLY PAYMENT/INCOME:
TOTAL INCOME	**$5,400.00**	31.24%
MONTHLY PAYMENT (P&I)	$1,448.65	TOTAL OBLIGATIONS/INCOME:
TAXES	208.33	35.87%
INSURANCE	30.00	COMMENTS:
OTHER	0.00	
TOTAL MONTHLY PAYMENT	**$1,686.98**	
OTHER OBLIGATIONS	250.00	
MONTHLY PMT & OBLIGATIONS	$1,936.98	

THESE FIGURES ARE TO BE USED AS ESTIMATES ONLY.

JOHN TERVEER:_____

313 N. SECOND AVE. * SUITE J * UPLAND, CA 91786
(714)981–1400

At loan application. When the loan application is finished, hand out extra business cards to the applicant and ask them to distribute them, or ask the applicant where they met "Mr. or Ms. Realtor." Upon their reply, ask, "Do you know many Realtors in the area?" You are establishing a referral network.

When introducing yourself or sending the first status report to the listing agent. After the Realtor says, "It's nice to meet an originator who feels that it's important to keep both Realtors informed," you respond with, "I haven't met many agents in your office, but would like a chance to meet you and some of the other agents in person. Perhaps I could take you and two or three other agents in your office to lunch?"

When the loan is settled. The last follow-up call after a "job well done" is a perfect place for a referral pitch. The applicant, settlement agent, and both Realtors are your targets.

Providing any "value added" service. Any time you provide something extra, you have leverage for a referral pitch. For example, after an open house for which you've provided a spread sheet, ask the agent for a visitor list, especially of Realtors. Call the Realtors and say, "I see that you visited Ms. Realtor's open house on Y Street this Sunday. I had the pleasure of providing mortgage information on the property with sample mortgage programs. What did you think of the presentation? Great, perhaps I can help you when you find the home for your customers or when you hold your next open house."

Referral opportunities are endless, limited only by the originator's imagination.

It's important to ask for referral letters from former applicants and Realtors you have serviced. If you've done a consistently good job for a Realtor, ask him or her to give you a letter recommending you to other agents. Sometimes applicants will even send unsolicited thank-you letters. When you meet a new Realtor who needs convincing, present previous customers' opinions about your level of service in the form of referral letters. The following exhibit is a dialogue you may use to get referrals.

Exhibit 4-18: Referrals

Situation: Back to the homebuyer after closing.

"John, my business is built on referrals. Could you name five people whom you respect and admire who can use my services?" (Immediately look down at your paper and be prepared to write.) Let the client speak first. (Do not look up.)

If the answer is "I don't remember anybody," say,
"How about at church?" (Look down at your paper.)
"How about at work?" (Look down at your paper.)

"Would you call ahead and refer me?"
If Yes, get commitment, date, and time.
If No, say, "Can I use your name?"

"In the meantime, if you can think of anyone else, jot their names down.

"I will call you back and tell you how everything went."

Go for more!

Exhibit 4-19: Sample Referral Letter

Joe Don
High Producing Realtor
High Producing Neighborhood

To Whom It May Concern:

The purpose of this letter is to recommend Tim Johns, an originator for ABC Mortgage Company.

I have known Tim for the past thirteen years and for the past five years have been referring him business as a Realtor. I am a high producer who cannot afford to spend my time involved in the mortgage approval process. Tim has handled over fifty transactions for me in the past five years—over $5 million in business—and I have never had any problems. He is professional and courteous, handles the applicants well, and, most of all, secures a quick approval time after time.

I wouldn't hesitate to use Tim on any transaction and I hope you will give him a try.

Sincerely,

Joe Don
Realtor

5

Time Management

In the interest of good service, originators tend to be drawn to the office and away from sales. Discipline is essential because originators manage their own time. How well they manage that time will, in large part, determine their sales capacity. It's not an exaggeration to say that efficient time management can be the difference between success and failure in mortgage sales.

Fortunately, there are tools to aid in time management as in any area of sales. We'll introduce these tools as we introduce the seven major steps to time management. To achieve your goals you must be able to juggle tasks and complete each efficiently. To manage time effectively you must:

- Plan
- Schedule
- Organize
- Prioritize
- Innovate
- Effectuate
- Evaluate

Set Short-Term and Intermediate Goals

To achieve success, you must plan every day, every week, and every month. Of course, to achieve success we must first define what we mean by success. We must define our short-term and intermediate goals. This isn't to say that long term goals are unimportant, but in daily life we focus on shorter-term objectives to direct our day-to-day actions. If achievement of these goals doesn't achieve our objectives in life, then perhaps we're performing in the wrong arena, or we're expecting too much from our environment.

Intermediate Goals

Our intermediate goals are comprehensive: annual production, annual income, breaking into a territory, and establishing positive name identification.

Our intermediate-term objectives are those upon which we direct our daily and weekly activities. In other words, we need to break intermediate objectives into short-term goals.

Exhibit 5-1:   Sample Goals

Annual production goal: $10,000,000

Average loan size: $100,000

Annual number of loans: 1000

Fallout rate: 10 percent

Number of originations per month: 11

Originations per week: 2.75

Monthly seasonal variations:

Jan.	Feb.	Mar.	April	May	June	July	Aug.	Sept.	Oct.	Nov.	Dec.
11	13	14	14	14	12	13	11	9	9	7	5

From here, we'll outline the steps necessary to achieve these monthly production figures. If your intermediate goal was income-based, we might add figures on overages and loan types. Breaking into certain offices or establishing relationships with particular agents are examples of target objectives.

Before we move to short-term goals, a few points regarding objective limits and tolerances. We should use historical information and market projections to set goals. In other words, you must consider both last year's production and the economic forecasts for the coming year.

While your goals should be realistic, they shouldn't be so conservative that they aren't challenging or they keep you from reaching your potential. If you set your goals too far from reality, you're unlikely to take the actions necessary to achieve them.

Short-Term Goals

Our translation of intermediate goals into short-term goals becomes our marketing plan. We must list the daily, weekly, and monthly actions that will help us attain longer-term objectives. For our production goal mentioned above, what actions will lead us to achieve our objectives?

- How many office visits?
- How many cold calls?
- How many mailings?
- How many lunches?
- How many sales meetings?
- How many seminars?
- What average approval turnaround figure?

The most important rule for goal achievement? Meet goals consistently, a step at a time. Three personal letters each day total over 1,000 each year. The following are ways to achieve consistency in your quest to meet your goals.

Schedule

Schedule everything necessary to help you achieve the goal. Originators typically schedule loan applications, prequalifications, and sales meetings. A major reason they don't meet office visit plans? They're not on the schedule.

We must block out office visits on our calendar. The same goes for status sessions with your processor, letter writing, and telephone prospecting. Also, schedule meetings with Realtors rather than dropping by. This saves time lost waiting and missing people. And it shows respect for the Realtor's time.

Organize

Scheduling is part of organizing, but only a small part. Scheduling is organizing our marketing plan, but we must go further. There is an extraordinary volume of information and paperwork in our industry. You must file and list this information so you can find it immediately.

File. Set up an organized filing system for program specifications, disclosures, forms, marketing materials, and operational memos. Taking 10 minutes a day to file these materials will save untold time otherwise spent calling your manager or underwriter with answers to questions.

List. Your daily plan should become a "things to do" list. There should be a one-page list for everything you must do in a day or week. Mountains of individual notes (some on the wall, some in your calendar, or several smaller lists) are hard to follow.

Prioritize

Now that you're organized and have your plan scheduled, you're ready to prioritize. Emergencies will arise that throw your schedule off. There's never enough time to perform every task on your list. When running short of time we typically:

- Respond to the "call of the wild." We react to tasks that scream the loudest, or we

- "Follow the path of least resistance," accomplishing pleasant tasks first, leaving the rougher tasks for later. We go to comfortable offices first, leaving the cold calls for last. Therefore, cold calls are forever pushed back. To be effective, attack cold calls when you are fresh.

A better approach is to establish priorities. An hour on the telephone selling a rate shopper might be less productive than lunch with a top producing real estate agent, but how much time do you spend in the office?

Exhibit 5-2:   Weekly Activities Schedule

	Mon	Tue	Wed	Thur	Fri	Sat	Sun
7:00 a.m.							
8:00							
9:00		Sales		Staff			
10:00	Off.1	Off.6	Off.4	Meeting			
11:00	Off.2	Off.7	Off.5	Sales	Off.9	Off.44	
12:00 noon	Off.3	Off.8		Meeting	Off.10	Applic.	
1:00 p.m.	Jim	Nat	R. Kitts	Status	Off.1	Off.6	Open
2:00					Off.2	App.	House
3:00	Off.4	Off.9	Off.1	Off.6	Prequal		
4:00	Off.5	Off.10	Off.2	Off.7	Off.3		
5:00			Off.3	Off.8			
6:00	Prequal	Applic.	Mailing	Follow-up			
7:00	Applic.			Calls			
8:00							

Here are my written goals for this week:

_____

_____

_____

_____

Exhibit 5-2 (Continued)

Cases to Lock:	Follow-up Calls:	Set-up Settlement:
Johnson	Land (Sell home)	Billings
Jones	Lawson (Coborrower)	Bozwell
James	Leads (Credit)	Binkney
Meetings to set up:		**Thank-you Notes**
Center (Broker)		Dennis
Forward (Attorney)		Downs
Left ($ Agent)		Dant

Innovate

It's true that an ambitious marketing plan and reasonable production level will leave us with too much to do in any particular day. But we know that the more tasks we accomplish, the more likely we are to achieve our intermediate objectives. To do this we must innovate. In time management, innovation means accomplishing as much as possible in as little time as possible, usually by performing two tasks with one action. It involves planning and organizing.

More than that, an originator strives to reach a high level of production and service it efficiently by developing and using various mechanisms. The following are areas ripe for mechanization:

- Setting up the loan application. Personally schedule the loan application, and don't meet with the applicant until they have the required documentation.

  Some originators, in their zeal for getting the loan, will meet with the applicant with little notice after the Realtor sets up the appointment. By calling the applicant personally and going over the items needed to process the application, you'll be able to submit the application and go on to the next task without spending days pursuing the information needed to finish the task and begin processing. This may delay application for a day or two until the applicant gets organized or co-applicants can appear together, but it's time efficient.

Realtors typically fail to communicate to the applicants the extent and importance of being prepared for loan application. One method of helping the Realtor prepare the applicant is to furnish the Realtor with application kits that walk applicants through the preparation process and help them organize information.

- Taking the loan application in the Realtor's office. Having the applicant come to your office for the loan application may seem time efficient, rather than traveling to the Realtor's office or the applicant's office or home. Yet, a problem for most originators is their inability to get out of the office and on the street.

  Combine taking the application in the Realtor's office with a marketing visit. Taking a loan application is an effective marketing visit and tool. It's good for Realtors to see how you handle their customers.

- Taking a complete loan application. We spoke previously about getting the information necessary to complete the application. Taking a complete loan application, i.e., filling in all the blanks and communicating all information in a well-organized manner to the processor, is a must.

  By submitting a complete loan application, you avoid wasting time with the processor going over the case, and it's less likely that mistakes will be made in processing. A consistent method of communicating with the processor helps organize the case. A complete log or status sheet can help in that regard.

- Get all underwriting questions answered up front. A good originator underwrites the case as he or she completes the loan application and answers all underwriting questions concerning case discrepancies. This eliminates (or at least reduces) surprises that crop up during processing and that may draw you into processing. Don't let it happen.

Originators spend untold hours rescuing cases and solving problems just before settlement. It's avoidable. Spend a few extra minutes reviewing the case and going over problems with a supervisor and underwriter.

Yes, this is another argument for your becoming an expert in product knowledge, plan specifications, and underwriting guidelines. Product knowledge is an integral part of a marketing plan.

- Status. A weekly status session with the processor saves time in many ways.

    a. A quick review of new mail can catch a problem the processor may have missed.

    b. Organize and plan the work necessary to process the caseload in such a way that you can "manage it from the road" the rest of the week. To do this, the processor and you must come up with a list that summarizes tasks: what needs to be done, who is to complete each task, by when is it to be completed and, if the workload is too heavy, will overtime or overflow help be necessary?

        The tasks themselves aren't outlined on the list because it's imperative to be able to view all necessary work on one page. There must be one list for both the processor and you. This allows you to touch base every day to communicate the items completed on the list, recognize tasks to be done, and add items as new applications come in and mail arrives.

        This organized system eliminates duplication, allows for planning, and makes good use of available resources.

c. Handcarrying a status report to the Realtor is time
    efficient because:

- The trip becomes a marketing visit which is
  more effective than delivering rate sheets. A status report is a marketing tool that helps you develop a relationship with the listing and selling
  agent.

- It's a positive communication that cuts down on
  status phone calls to you and the processor. In
  other words, if you don't spend your time on
  this positive marketing effort, you'll spend the
  time on the phone giving out the information,
  often defensively.

- It's a way to eliminate making phone calls. You
  will otherwise have to call the Realtor to ask for
  information or ask for help in getting the applicant to respond. Writing notes directly on the
  status report eliminates Realtor "telephone tag."

If your origination system isn't automated, you can save
time by providing Realtors copies of your processor com-
munications log (as a makeshift status sheet). This involves
spending more time completing it neatly and keeping it
clear, but saves time overall.

- Developing an organized marketing plan. This plan should
  include the information necessary to become knowledgeable about the target area and major players. It prevents
  wasted effort in territory development and uncoordinated
  and haphazard marketing efforts. See the sample marketing plan exhibit.

- Don't go to the office in the morning to organize a loan
  application taken the night before. Finish organizing the
  loan application (filling out qualification sheets, the registration sheet, and status log or communication form) directly after you take the loan application.

Organize the material in the Realtor's office or at home. This way application details are fresh in your mind, and you can fill out forms as the applicant reads disclosures and other forms.

Loan applications may last a few extra minutes if you combine the task of finishing internal forms with the loan application itself. But if you go into the office, you'll answer phone calls, get involved in conversations, and lose hours of time. At a minimum, you should finish the application before you leave the house in the morning. Your trip to the office should solely be to drop off the application.

- Return phone calls from Realtors' offices. Instead of staying in the office and returning calls, return them from your target offices. This way you'll be interrupted only by Realtors with qualification questions and other concerns, and avoid being pulled into operations at your office.

For cold calls and unfamiliar offices, asking to use the phone to return a page is a way to get past the receptionist's desk. Again, having Realtors watch you in action is a marketing tool in itself.

- Research before you sell. Do a market analysis of your territory's needs and key players before you sell. This information state of sales keeps you from wasting time trying to sell the wrong products or the wrong players.

You may gravitate to those who are easier to approach, yet the approachable have free time because they aren't busy selling or listing homes. If you learn your target's needs before you try to sell, matching products to those needs makes for fast closes.

- Ask for the business up front. Find out at the beginning whether a target can do business with you. Don't spend weeks or months working a Realtor to find there's no way that person will refer a mortgage to you due to prior commitments, circumstances, or whatever.

You should get this information during the first visit after you assessed the Realtor's needs. (Remember, asking for the business up front doesn't mean asking for the business before you analyze needs and determine the best way to fill them.)

- Constantly target prior customers. You spent alot of time selling realtors and applicants when you accomplished a loan, prequalification open house, or other function. Improper follow-up negates this effort.

    Don't spend all of your time selling new targets. If you've done a good job for a Realtor, you're 98 percent of the way to the next loan application. And, of course, referrals from the satisfied Realtor and applicant are solid marketing tools.

- Combine marketing efforts when possible. Think through every marketing effort to identify all potential applications, and follow up. Here's what we mean:

    a. Providing an open house spread sheet. The spread sheet helps the Realtor. Don't hesitate to ask for a list of visitors, especially other Realtors.

    b. Writing a newsletter. The newsletter is a "value added" education-related marketing tool. Used it as a vehicle for obtaining seminars and sales meetings, as a mailing, and to familiarize an unfamiliar office with you and your company before making a sales call.

- Combine phone calls. Don't call your processor, underwriter, or supervisor every time you have a question. Save your questions for one call per day. This will save countless minutes otherwise spent holding and leaving messages.

    A good example of this is the one per day status call with the processor to go over the status list and the day's mail, and to plan the next day.

- Make use of driving time. An originator spends many hours each week in his or her car. Combine this time with other tasks.

  a.   If you have a car phone, make calls from the car so you don't lose time when you arrive at your destination.

  b.   Listen to sales, motivation talk, and other self-help instructional tapes while driving. You can listen to a six-hour sales course in just a few days while driving. You can't take notes, but you can listen to the tapes repeatedly for retention.

  c.   Evaluate sales calls and plan the next call while driving. Don't listen to music between calls. Evaluate what happened. Did you achieve your objectives? What must you do to follow up? How should you change your approach for the next office?

  d.   Use a dictaphone to record ideas and letters that need to go out.

  Innovation is an endless endeavor. Think about what occupies your time during a normal working day and determine how you can accomplish these tasks more efficiently and, more important, how you can combine tasks to accomplish two or more objectives.

Effectuate

Effectuate means get the job done. All the planning, scheduling, organizing, and innovating in the world won't help if you don't act.

- Finish one task at a time. Though a single task may accomplish several objectives, don't try to work on many tasks at a time. This is a blueprint for accomplishing nothing. Finish one task before moving to another, even if you must

fend off such interruptions as phone calls. Allow enough
time between loan applications to finish one before you
begin another.

- Finish the work. No matter how many fires come up during the day, make sure you finish the work on your list
before the day is complete. This may mean a few extra
hours, but it will prevent spending days or weeks catching
up on routine tasks. Spend 10 minutes filing at the end of
the day, every day, and make sure you return every phone
call by the end of the day. Otherwise, you'll begin the next
day catching up on yesterday.

Evaluate

At the end of the day, evaluate what you've accomplished. If you
didn't finish your list, why not? How might you eliminate the
items that came up? Should you amend the list? Are you spending
too much time on non-priorities?

Write down everything you've accomplished. How much time
should every task have taken? What caused "planning vs. reality"
gaps? Are you trying to accomplish too much? Time management
calls for constant feedback and re-evaluation. The planning process must be constant.

In addition, long-term evaluation is significant. Are you
achieving intermediate objectives? How must you alter your marketing plan? Use regular staff meetings and meetings with your
peers and supervisor for evaluation. Be prepared to present your
progress so you can have the benefit of an evaluation. This way,
you'll be making good use of meeting and other administrative
time.

Exhibit 5-3:   Time Management Reality Check

Originator: _____ Date: _____

Accomplished:

Number	Task	Time Elapsed	Planned
_____	Loan Applications	_____	75 minutes each
_____	Prequalifications	_____	15 minutes each
_____	Rate Sheet Prep.	_____	15 minutes
_____	Rate Calls	_____	5 minutes each
_____	Spread Sheets	_____	30 minutes each
_____	Sales Calls	_____	45 minutes each
_____	Staff Meetings	_____	2 hours each week
_____	Status/Processing	_____	1 hour each day
_____	Travel Time	_____	2 hours each day
_____	Marketing Meeting/ Sales Presentation	_____	2 hours each day
_____	Mailings	_____	2 hours each week (10 minutes each)
_____	Prospect Calls	_____	30 minutes each day
_____	Total	_____	_____

Does planning meet reality?

Exhibit 5-4:   Loan Originator Reality Check

Assess the individual skills you bring to your daily responsibilities. Unfortunately, loan originators are often so busy putting out fires and handling any number of crises that they don't have time to assess the ways in which they approach their business opportunities and volume generation.

Loan Originator Skill: Phase I
Your Level of Productivity   Date:_____

                                          Weak   OK   Strong

1. Meeting target production goals quarterly.

---

2. Maintaining existing customer base.

---

3. Generating volume from new services.

---

4. Creating and benefitting from an ongoing referral network program.

Loan Originator Skill: Phase I
Degree of Customer Base Penetration   Date:_____

                                          Weak   OK   Strong

1. Targeting the top 10 percent of Realtors in your marketing area.

---

2. Builder/Developer penetration.

---

3. Penetrating the available market to the degree determined by
    branch/unit goals.

Exhibit 5-4   (Continued)

Loan Originator Skill: Phase I
Business Management   Date:_____

                               Weak   OK   Strong

1. Keeping expenditures within budget.

2. Turning in quality reports in a timely manner.

3. Acquiring appropriate and current market/competition information.

4. Ensuring customer satisfaction.

5. Managing time and territory effectively.

6. Creating special projects:
   a. Seminars
   b. Outside speaking engagements

Loan Originator Skill: Phase I
Selling Skill   Date:_____

                               Weak   OK   Strong

1. Maximizing pre-call research opportunities.

2. Thorough needs analysis.

Exhibit 5-4   (Continued)

3. Effectively handling objections.

---

4. Asking for the business/commitment.

---

5. Utilization of feature/benefit selling.

---

6. Setting yourself apart from the competition.

Loan Originator Skill: Phase I
Customer Services   Date:_____

                                          Weak   OK   Strong

1. Telephone calls promptly returned.

---

2. Thorough needs analysis.

---

3. Regular use of a follow-up system.

---

4. Thoroughness of explanations without setting the blame.

---

5. Appreciative attitude.

Exhibit 5-5: Daily Objectives

Date:_____

Things to do	Telephone calls	Appointments

Who deserves praise?
Who needs coaching?
What should I think about?

"Put off till tomorrow . . . things that shouldn't be done at all."

Exhibit 5-6:   Monthly Office Goal Planner

Originator:_____Month:_____

Office/Builder	# of Calls	Applications	Pre-Quals	Meetings
_____	_____	_____	_____	_____
_____	_____	_____	_____	_____
_____	_____	_____	_____	_____
_____	_____	_____	_____	_____
_____	_____	_____	_____	_____
_____	_____	_____	_____	_____
_____	_____	_____	_____	_____
_____	_____	_____	_____	_____

Additional Goals:

Cold Calls: _____   Office Mailings: _____
Closings: _____ Number: _____ Volume: _____

Exhibit 5-7:   Status Log

Date: _____

Work Ups:	Underwriting Conditions:
1. Jones (P) Friday	1. Johnson (P) Thursday
2. Eds (P) Monday	2. West (P) Tuesday
3. John (P) Monday	3. East (O) Thursday
4.	4.
5.	5.
6.	6.

Follow Ups:	Set Ups:
1. Tims (O) Thursday	1. Pats (P) Friday
2. Rich (P) Thursday	2. Janet (P) Friday
3. James (P) Monday	3.
4. Perry (O) Thursday	4.
5. Eisen (O) Thursday	5.
6.	6.

Settlement Dates Needed:	Loans to Lock:
1. Jones (O) Thursday	1. Jones (O) Thursday
2. Johnson (P) Weds.	2. James (O) Weds.
3. Jameson (P) Friday	3. Jameson (O) Thursday
4.	4.
5.	5.
6.	6.

Exhibit 5-7 (Continued)

Phone Calls: Misc.:

1 Rich's Appraisal (P) Thursday   1. Tim's Tax Return Review
                                                    (O) Weekend

2. James (P) Thursday   2.

3. Edwards (P) Thursday   3.

4. Tom's Attorney (P) Thursday   4.

5. Jim's Accountant (O) Thursday   5.

6.   6.

O = originator
P = processor

Exhibit 5-8: Loan Officer Personal Production Log

Year _____ Page _____

DATE	NAME	LOAN AMT	PROG. #	RATE	PTS.	EXP. DATE	APPR	- / + %	PROJ. CLOSING	ACTUAL CLOSING	SELLING AGENT/ OFFICE	LISTING AGENT/ OFFICE

6

Overcoming Objections and Moving to the Close

Objections

No matter how well you prepare your clients with information, you'll meet objections. Objections can be a frightening development to any salesperson. After all, your target's telling you why he or she won't do business with you. It's easy to take objections as personal criticism rather than the necessary stage of sales that they are. Don't.

Why are objections a necessary stage of sales? They're part of the information stage. At this point the person is telling you what you must do to close. If you can't overcome the objection (and this will happen), move to the next target.

As a consultative salesperson, you should spend as much time as possible learning how to overcome objections to get to a close. There are two important things to remember about objections.

- There are a few basic rules for dealing with objections. Follow those rules to overcome any specific objection.

223

- There's a limit to the types of objections you'll meet. In originations, there are only five possible objections. (We'll discuss some of these in this chapter.)

The basic rules of objections:

- Ask for the business. You'll never learn the real reasons why a Realtor or applicant won't do business with you unless you ask for the business. If you aren't being presented with objections, you aren't asking for the business. A Realtor won't volunteer information unless you put that person on the spot with, "Why won't you do business with me?"

- Listen. Remember, the key to relationships is to be a good listener. If you don't listen carefully to the objection, you'll appear indifferent to the problem. This is an important time for affirmative and sympathetic body language.

- Repeat the objection. You must repeat the objection to be sure you understand it. It's too easy to misconstrue the objection or steer it toward a familiar or achievable arena. Make sure the Realtor acknowledges that you've recognized and understood the objection.

  "Let me see if I understand you correctly. You feel that we're priced too high, is that correct?"

- Don't argue. Agree, and show sympathy to Realtors' concerns. "I appreciate your concern for . . ."

  Arguing is no way to begin a relationship. The key to salesmanship is to persuade without conflict or to change Realtors' minds by saying that they were right all along. Basically, you want to show Realtors that your response to their objections is a reason why they should do business with you.

- Ask questions. Asking questions is the essence of listening and sales. The issue may resolve itself through further investigation. For example, perhaps the delayed settlement a Realtor experienced previously wasn't your company's fault, or the situation has been resolved. You may learn specifics that will help you overcome the objection now and in the future. If the Realtor works with a certain originator, why? What business or functions are beyond your capacity? Does the Realtor need a backup?

- Don't try to resolve all objections. There will be some objections you can't resolve at first, or ever. Recognize both situations, because trying to resolve an objection at the wrong time will lead to arguments, frustration, and a waste of time. If you agree that an objection is important and you can't overcome it, move on quickly and professionally. (But ask for referrals!)

- Be prepared. Since you'll meet a limited number of objections, it's simple to prepare possible questions and responses. Overcoming an objection is a sales presentation you must prepare and practice religiously. Again, the key to any presentation is preparation.

Basic Objections

There are a few categories of objection types, though they may be worded differently. These categories call for the same approach. We will present them as follows:

- Price
- Product
- Loyalty
- Unfamiliarity
- Prejudice

Price

Price is a major objection in any sales field. It's important to note that many applicants will make their decision based solely on price. Car dealers vary in price, yet some customers are loyal to certain dealers, and others shop around to save one hundred dollars.

True price shoppers present an objection you can't overcome unless you have the lowest or close to the lowest rate in town. Even getting the application may not represent true success because price purists are known for filing dual applications (floating one and locking the other), or demanding a new lock when rates go down. You can't truly sell rate shoppers. Because you'll have the lowest rate in town only a small percentage of the time, it's important not to dwell on rate rejection. Rate rejection is going to happen often. Rate shoppers call everyone. How should you handle the price objection?

- Avoid price idolaters. If someone tells you that their most important or only selection factor is price, then accept the message. All too often a Realtor will ask you to cut your price to make a deal, and you'll do so to break in with that Realtor or that office. The problem is that *no repeat business is forthcoming* unless you have the lowest price the next time.

Let us assume that the world is divided accordingly:

Price Only	Price and Other Factors	Loyalty
33%	33%	33%

The message here is to avoid the 33 percent and attack the other 67 percent. There's your market share. Don't spend an inordinate amount of time selling someone who won't be loyal anyway. In addition, many times Realtors and homebuyers will identify price as the important decision factor or as a major objection. Don't accept this information without a "smokeout" of questions to make sure that they're "price only's." Otherwise, 33 percent becomes 67 percent, limiting your market share.

- Sell products that don't lend themselves to price competition. Some of these products are actually services.

Rather than advocating a certain price or product, promote a service that provides the security of knowing what the homebuyer can afford up front, speeds settlements, and gives the homebuyer leverage with the seller. While there remains the possibility that your client will price shop after they sign a contract, the chance will be lessened.

Here are examples of such products and services:

Pre-purchase loan programs. These programs invite applications before the home is purchased. You avoid the rate dilemma because you bring the loan in before rate becomes an issue.

Rate cap programs. Many companies have programs that cap rather than lock rates. These allow the rate to float down with the protection of a rate ceiling. If your competition is selling "today's rate" and you are selling a "capped rate," you avoid direct comparison.

Buydowns. Many companies are now providing quotes on standard 2-1 or 1-0 temporary buydown programs. But you can offer a 1 1/2–1/2 buydown or any other allowable combination. Getting away from the mainstream limits price competitors. Buydowns can be tailored to individual needs or to compete against specific programs, such as a three-year ARM.

Closing costs financed. Selling the advantages of financing closing costs by taking on a higher rate also circumvents direct comparison. The majority of lenders quote at an origination fee at the very least.

Growing Equity Mortgages and BiWeeklys. There are a variety of programs for specific purposes and they vary from a standard "fixed rate" quote.

- Make sure all information is available. All too often the originator hears a competitor's quote over the phone and attempts frantically to match it. However, it's common for quotes to be outdated, to apply to a slightly different product (such as a 7-year balloon rather than a 30-year fixed), to have hidden costs, or to be the product of another originator's speculation.

Always ask the name of the company and independently verify the quote. Also, make sure you have enough information about the applicant's situation and needs.

The homebuyer or Realtor may have asked for a no-income/no-asset program quote, but needed only the no-income verification program which may have a lower rate. The other company may have taken the time and effort to ask and make the adjustment without informing the shopper.

- Isolate the price issue. Make sure the shopper knows exactly how much the difference in price represents. For example, it's common for a shopper to make a loan placement decision on the basis of one-quarter of one point (0.25 percent).

If the loan amount is $80,000, the decision has been made on the basis of $200. Total closing costs may be $6,000 and payments over the life of the loan $300,000. This puts $200 in perspective.

This is the time to let the Realtor know what your services are worth. If he or she doesn't agree that a professional who is striving for a long-term relationship is worth $200 extra, then you may have a true price shopper who cannot be sold on any other basis.

Product

You may confuse a product objection with a loyalty objection unless you use some basic questioning techniques. When a Realtor or borrower says, "I only work with Mike Jones or Low Mortgage," you respond with, "Why? What is it about them that makes you give them your business?"

The client may identify a specific program Mike offers. You must find out why the program is important to show how you can accomplish the same or more with a different or similar program.

"You say that you only do business with Mike Jones, is that right?"

"Yes."

"What is it about Mike, or what does he offer to earn your business?"

"Mike has a program that has the security of a fixed rate but qualifies my homebuyers for 20 percent more house than a fixed rate."

"I can see where this program would be significant. What is it called?"

"It is a 2-1 Buydown with Low Points."

"Where is the quote today?"

"8%-9%-10% 1+1 for a conforming loan amount."

"If I can show you a program that accomplishes the same objective and can be tailor-made for each individual buyer, would you be interested in hearing about it?"

The point here is to be prepared to match programs, feature for feature, benefit for benefit. Possible benefits include:

- qualifying for more house
- security of a fixed rate or payment
- more affordable rate or payments
- building up more equity
- making more money (Realtor sells larger or more homes, and the homebuyer gets the advantage of greater leverage)

Translate features into target benefits. To overcome a product objection, one must match benefit to benefit, not feature to feature. Use transition phrases such as "which means to you" or "therefore, you." Selling benefits allows you to overcome realtor product objections, "which means to you" more originations.

Loyalty

Loyalty is an opportunity, yet presents an obstacle. If a Realtor cites loyalty to a particular company or originator, you have identified the type of Realtor you'd like to service: the 33 percent who make decisions independent of price.

It's simple to find out what the Realtor's favorite is doing right—ask why he or she uses that particular originator or company. What could the reasons be?

- Price (which puts the realtor in the middle 33 percent)
- Reliability
- Knowledge
- Friendship or other relationship (the originator may be his or her spouse!)
- Experience
- Other services the company provides
- Institutional relationship (real estate owned mortgage company)
- Product (we've already covered this)

Don't try to convince the realtor that relationships and loyalty aren't important. If you ask to be a back-up lender, you may wind up being referred the "dog loans" that the other company couldn't approve.

Study the competitor. What can you do that they can't? For example, you may have a three-year adjustable and they don't. If you've studied your major competitors during the information stage, you'll be able to point out the difference at once. If not, let the Realtor know that you appreciate their loyalty, but just the same if you find such a niche, you'll be back to them.

Unfamiliarity

The Realtor simply may not have heard of you or your company. Realtors don't like the "new kid." This objection is easy to overcome if you've prepared an introductory package, especially one that includes referral letters.

You can avoid this objection altogether by using mailing techniques to introduce yourself and your company before you make the call. If you've sent direct mail for a month before your first visit, there will be some degree of familiarity.

Another method of getting around the unfamiliarity objection is to use a referral system. If the introduction is made through a referral or mutual acquaintance, barriers fall. However, not every company or originator will be known by everyone and personal introductions aren't always possible. Here you must attack the objection through concentrated efforts.

- Ask the Realtor for time to go over the introductory package. Lunch is a good idea.

- Secure an invitation to a sales meeting in that office.

- Bombard the Realtor and office with mailings, flyers, and newsletters for a while. Make several office visits in a short time.

Prejudice

What are common prejudices?

- You're inexperienced.

- Your company has a bad reputation.

- I've had a bad experience with your company.

With regard to inexperience, one must look at the word "experienced" in context. It's rare that someone becomes an originator without some experience in real estate, mortgage banking, or sales.

Emphasize broad experience rather than the lack of specific origination experience. Saying, "I've been involved in 300 real estate transactions over the past five years" is more convincing than, "I have never originated before, but I was previously a real estate agent." There will be some of you who don't fit into any experi-

ence category (just out of college, for example). Here you have two
choices:

- Look for someone to give you a "first shot" and build on
  these successes through referrals.

- Perform a variety of services for the Realtor to convince
  him or her of your competence: seminars, open house
  spread sheets, prequalifications, and newsletters.

In the case of problems with negative reputation or experience, use questioning skills to isolate the incident or issue so you
can address it. Find out what exactly happened from the Realtor's
viewpoint, then find out what really happened from your
company's viewpoint. (Remember, there are two sides to every
issue.)

If there was a specific problem, show that it was corrected (for
example, "That person is no longer with the company"). Even if
you don't think your company committed a grievous error, don't
correct the Realtor (unless he or she wasn't aware of a third party
that caused the problem). Apologize and ask for another chance to
show your and your company's actual level of service.

The following exhibits contain actual responses to objections
supplied by industry experts in origination sales. Again, the key to
overcoming objections is to know the objections you'll encounter
in advance and practice, practice, practice the appropriate response.

Exhibit 6-1:   Objections

1. "You're New and Inexperienced"
    "Mr. Client, you're very successful in your business. I'm sure there was a time when you first started that you had very little experience. Someone gave you the chance to prove yourself and all I am asking from you is for you to give me that same chance. To conserve your time and see how I can be of maximum benefit to you, may I ask you a few questions?"

2. "Rates, points or fees are too high."
    "We may not always have the lowest rates in town, but we close our loans in _____ days which means you save time, which, of course, is money."

3. I need to go where I can find the lowest possible rates."

    "Sure. I understand that you have to find the best possible deal for your buyers. Every really good Realtor feels that way. Many of them find, however, that the lower rate carries with it higher fees. Or the lender gets loaded up with too much business, and can't get it all funded on schedule, or there are special underwriting qualifications to consider that may sour the deal.
    "With us, you'll always get a fair price for your clients, with the assurance of my personal best with every transaction. You'll never have to worry about what you are giving up, to save a little on the rate."

4. "You're priced too high."
    "Let me see if I understand. You feel that we're priced too high, is that correct? I can see why getting the best price you can is important to you. You do want to be sure that you've got the best deal for yourself, don't you? There are many lenders in town. Who have you compared us to? What was the quote they provided you? As you can see, there are many factors that affect the overall price of a loan. Does this make sense to you?"

From Debra Jones, "The Mortgage Generator"

Exhibit 6-2: Selling Against the Competition

Features	Program	Program	Program
Annual Percentage Rate (APR)	_____	_____	_____
Adjustable Rate Mortgage (ARM)	_____	_____	_____
Assumable	_____	_____	_____
Buydowns	_____	_____	_____
Conversion	_____	_____	_____
Fixed	_____	_____	_____
Graduated Payments	_____	_____	_____
Index	_____	_____	_____
Loan Fee	_____	_____	_____
Lock Ins	_____	_____	_____
Margin	_____	_____	_____
Mortgage Insurance	_____	_____	_____
Negative Amortization	_____	_____	_____
Payment Cap	_____	_____	_____
Prepayment Penalty	_____	_____	_____
Rate	_____	_____	_____
Rate Cap	_____	_____	_____
Term	_____	_____	_____
80% LTV	_____	_____	_____
90% LTV	_____	_____	_____

Exhibit 6-3: Flush Out Hidden Costs

Annual Percentage Rate (APR)

How is the APR computed?

What charges did you use to calculate APR? (For example, some lenders include the discount paid by the seller on an FHA loan and some include mortgage insurance.)

Adjustable Rate Mortgages (ARMs)

Review the FNMA ARM brochure.

Assumable

Is the loan assumable to anybody at anytime?

Is it "at the lender's option" and subject to paragraph 17 of the FNMA Deed of Trust?

Is it assumable, as is, or will the rate be increased at the time of the assumption?

What fees are involved?

Is the assumability provision lost after a conversion option is exercised?

Buydowns

Does a buydown make sense for the buyer? Will the extra initial cost pay for itself in payment savings during the time he or she expects to own the property?

Will the buydown help the borrower qualify?

Will the lender qualify the buyer at the buydown rate, the note rate, or a rate in-between?

Is it a permanent buydown?

Is it a temporary buydown?

What is the term of the buydown?

Exhibit 6-3   (Continued)

Is there a maximum limit to the buydown?

Most important, what is the justification or reason for buying down? Is it a pay me now or pay me later situation?

Note: A buydown may make sense if there is an excess of points paid by the seller or if the buyer wants to qualify at a lower interest rate.

Conversion

When can the conversion be made? Anniversary date or anytime?

At what cost?

How long is the option available?

At what rate will the conversation be made? At best available current fixed rate or will the rate be increased?

"No fee"—Is that no loan fee or does it mean no fees whatever? Does the buyer have to pay third party costs (credit report and title report)? Does the buyer have to requalify at the time of conversion?

What determines the rate the buyer will convert to? (Usually described in an adjustable rate rider.)

Fixed Rate

Is there a prepayment charge?

Is the loan assumable?

Must the property be owner-occupied?

What is the maximum loan-to-value ratio?

Does the loan require mortgage insurance?

Can you waive the reserve requirement by making a larger down payment?

Exhibit 6-3   (Continued)

Graduated Payment

Does the loan negatively amortize? If it doesn't, what happens?

How much discount must be paid?

Is it a Growing Equity Mortgage (GEM)? It may start with a fixed rate and rise from there.

Might it be helpful to take a fixed-rate loan and make it your own GEM? (For example, on a 30-year fixed-rate loan, if the borrower chooses to make additional payments of $100 to principal each month, the loan could be paid off in 15 years.)

The following payment schedule illustrates this advantage:

$ 50,000 @ 12%, 30 year, 360 payments = 514.31 P & I

$ 100 additional each month = 614.31 P & I

The 360 months become 169 months for a total savings of 514.31 × 191 months or $98,233.21

Index

What index is being used?

How is it being computed?

Does it accurately reflect the lender's cost of funds?

How quickly does it react to changes in the market?

What is its history?

Will the lag time for increases and decreases in the market be the same? If not, what happens?

Which movement would show up first, an increase or decrease?

What is the margin? The index can become a less significant factor because of the margin or spread.

What is the customer's understanding of the index?

What will the interest rate be if the index doesn't change by the first adjustment?

Exhibit 6-3   (Continued)

Loan Fee—Additional Fees

What does the loan fee include?

Are there additional "garbage fees"?

What's the relationship between your interest rate and loan fee and theirs?

Is the buyer or Realtor focusing on loan fee? Is there more to take into consideration than just the loan origination cost?

Does the loan fee include a first-year mortgage insurance?

Lock-ins

What is the time period for the lock-in?

Why does the buyer want one?

What is the cost?

Does the lock-in fix that rate for a period of time?

Does the lock-in allow any downturn advantage during the lock-in period?

Is there a fee for the lock-in, and is it refundable at time of closing?

Is the lock-in in writing?

Is the lock-in valid if the buyer, seller, property, or loan amount changes?

Margin

To what index is the margin added?

What is the margin?

Can the margin be discounted or bought down?

If the index shows a rate increase or decrease, is it mandatory or at lender's option?

If the lender decides not to impose an increase, can it be imposed later?

Exhibit 6-3   (Continued)

Negative Amortization

Is negative amortization limited? To what amount?

If the maximum allowable negative amortization is reached, how will it affect the original terms of the loan?

Mortgage Insurance (MI)

At what loan-to-value is MI required?

Are the MI rates competitive within the market place?

Can the up-front premium be financed?

Prepayment Charge

Is there a prepayment charge?

Does it apply to the total prepayment, partial prepayment or both?

If a partial prepayment, is there a minimum or maximum amount that can be prepaid?

Is it for the life of the loan or for a limited period?

Rate Cap—Payment Cap

Does the loan provide reasonable caps to prevent potential "payment shock"?

Are there caps on the discounted rate, note rate, or both?

Could any of the caps potentially cause negative amortization?

Is there a lifetime cap on rate?

Do both annual and lifetime caps apply to decreases as well as increases? Is there a floor or minimum rate?

Are the caps based upon a teaser rate or the note rate?

Can increases in the index beyond the rate cap be carried over to subsequent years?

Exhibit 6-3   (Continued)

"Teaser" Rate

What is the initial note rate? How much of the teaser rate has been discounted?

What is the margin?

What is the term of the teaser rate?

Are there any caps on the first adjustment?

What will the monthly payment be at the first adjustment?

Term

What is the term of the loan?

How will the difference in term affect the borrower's ability to qualify?

Will a different term fulfill the buyer's particular needs?

Can the buyer adequately handle the increase in monthly payment amount resulting from a shorter term?

Can the term of the loan be extended to longer than 30 years? What are the potential benefits?

Part of your formula for success as a loan officer includes taking the initiative to understand the complexities of the mortgage market, specifically your competitor's programs.

Closing

Closing the sale is an extension of asking for business. As a consultative salesperson, your objective is to answer objections during the information stage. This reduces the time between asking and closing. If you ask for something and there are no objections, the time to close is now. If objections remain, you must overcome them.

Closing reluctance is as prevalent as call reluctance. An originator who asks for the business, yet is conditioned to hear No may not know what to say when there is a Yes. More than any other facet of sales, closing isn't learned, it's instinctive. Closing statements are relatively simple.

"Would you like to meet on Tuesday or Thursday evening?" (alternative)

"Would you like to lock in before we meet?" (assumptive)

"Rates are going up, we'd better get going. Is Wednesday okay?" (reference to an impending event)

It isn't hard to learn these simple phrases. The trick is to ask questions with Yes answers. You can rephrase the simple question, "Can I have your next loan?" to "So we have a basis for doing business?" or "Would you like me to do the loan application in my office or yours?" These restatements are more positive.

If these closes are so simple, then what is the problem? Well, the secret to closing is *timing*. You must recognize closing situations and when it's the right time in that situation to close. And closing situations aren't limited to getting a loan. We close for all of our objectives, whether our goal is scheduling a lunch or sales meeting.

It's difficult to teach timing. This is what we mean by saying someone is a born salesperson. Some salespersons say all the right things, yet never convince someone to do business with them. Others can do it time and time again. It's like telling a joke. Two people can tell the same joke and get entirely different reactions. The difference is in the delivery, and much of this delivery depends on timing.

You can't practice timing at home. You must be out there trying to recognize closing situations. Going out with an experienced originator is a good idea. Closings happen all around us—any time that you want someone to do something. Closing statements happen in sales meetings and in social situations. An example of a difficult closing situation is asking for a first date.

Someone who is persuasive isn't someone who argues constantly, but someone who closes effectively. It's the action that pulls the whole plan together. We can place closing situations in the following categories:

- The Realtor and the real estate office.

- Getting an appointment.

- Getting an application.

The Realtor and the Real Estate Office

From the time you walk through the door of a real estate office you will be presented with closing situations.

- Getting past the Receptionist or Deputy Agent.

- Obtaining permission to hand out sheets personally rather than "stuff the box."

- Obtaining a few minutes of someone's time.

- Getting a commitment from a Realtor to work with you.

- Getting a Receptionist to let you know when contracts are written.

Getting An Appointment

Here are situations that entail setting up a meeting (other than a loan application).

- Setting up an appointment to meet with a Realtor, his or her client, or the Sales Manager.

- Setting up lunch with a Realtor, Sales Manager, or Receptionist.

- Setting up a sales meeting.
- Setting up a seminar.
- Turning a rate shopper into an appointment.

Getting the Loan Application

This is your goal. What are the situations to garner a loan application? Any appointment with a client can become a loan application.

- Getting a commitment for the next loan application from a Realtor.
- Turning a pre-qualification into a pre-approval loan application.
- Generating a loan application from a rate shopper.

There are myriad situations to ask for a loan application. The trick is to close at the right time—not early or late.

Timing

The most obvious ill-timed closing is one attempted too early.

"Hi, my name is Sam Sleaze from Sleaze Mortgage. Can I have your next loan?"

This sounds ridiculous. Just as ridiculous is someone who waits too long, someone who asks for the business at an appropriate period, answers all objections, and then rambles on for minutes afterwards until the Realtor thinks, "There is no way I am doing business with someone who talks this much!"

A good close is one that *identifies a need* and *presents a solution*. Your potential client must apply immediately. Create a sense of urgency, even if it is ever so slight.

"You have to close in 30 days? We'd better get started right away! I have one appointment available this evening. Would 8:00 pm be alright with you?"

"You say the seller is paying only two points and you have just enough cash to cover the loan origination fee and down payment? We need to get you rate protection immediately. How quickly can we meet?"

It isn't always possible to create a sense of urgency, but excitement in your voice shows that you recognize this is a significant event in their life, and this excitement helps you deliver a close.

"This is your first home? Congratulations! I know you consider this an important step for your financial goals, and it's important to consider all alternatives available so you may take full advantage of this opportunity. I would like to work out some numbers on several loan plans that we will tailor to your financial situation. Would you like to meet this Friday?"

Regardless of the urgency of the situation and the sense of excitement you convey, you must identify their needs and show them how you can fill them before the close. This is why you're always ready to sum up the benefits of any particular program at a moment's notice. What are the *needs* of someone you approach in a closing situation?

Duty Agent: Important news concerning change in mortgage programs, to prequalify someone who has just called in.

Agent: Qualify more customers, sell a listing, increase business, convert a shopper into a buyer, quick settlement.

New Agent: Training in financing.

Manager: Training for new agents, a good speaker, new mortgage program that will increase business, important news.

Homebuyer: Qualify, low rate or payments, save interest, build equity, low downpayment, quick settlement.

These needs are easily recognizable. By distinquishing between the benefits of each of your programs, you'll be able to cross the bridge from need to closing quickly and efficiently, with good timing. Here are a few examples:

"You say you're interested in building equity as quickly as possible, is that true? We have several mortgage options that achieve accelerated equity objectives, including the standard 15-year fixed, Biweekly Mortgages, 20-year amortization, and a Growing Equity Mortgage. I think it would be important to go over each of these alternatives in detail, don't you agree? Would tomorrow evening be o.k.?"

"You're new in the business? Congratulations, I know you'll find the real estate business very challenging. What areas of financing have you found the most difficult to absorb? All of it? We have an excellent training session which covers basic programs and qualifying. Sometimes an individual session can bring more understanding than learning in a group training environment, don't you agree? Why don't we meet . . ."

"FHA has just made some major changes in requirements for qualifying. These new rules will affect how we approach the marginally qualified FHA buyer. It's important that agents become familiarized with the new rules as soon as possible, don't you agree? We have prepared a summary that takes only five minutes to go over. Would you like me to present it at your next sales meeting?"

"Your say that your agent has informed you that you'll need an adjustable-rate mortgage to qualify for the house? Is that the type of mortgage you would like to have? There are several new programs that actually replicate the qualification characteristics of an adjustable yet add the safety of long-term fixed rates. Wold you like to hear more about them? Let's meet Tuesday to discuss them."

The examples are endless. The important point to remember is that you must use your questioning skills to locate client needs, match them with the benefits you offer, and move directly to the close. This sequence must be automatic. Match and close, it's that simple. Memorize closes, recognize needs, and know every product and client benefit you have to offer.

You must be able to manipulate the conversation to achieve this sequence. You can't memorize this art of conversation, you must perform it day in and day out. Without the close, all the preparation in the world won't make a sale happen.

Sales Training
Available in the Industry

There is a wide range of sales training tools available in the mortgage industry. This chapter summarizes courses available and contains instructor backgrounds and contact information. These experts contributed a large portion of this book.

It's important to note that these courses are not the only ones available—each of the organizations listed has seminars and sales materials on topics from customer service to sales management training.

This information is subject to change, and the the Mortgage Bankers Association doesn't directly endorse the courses.

Jack Davis—
Selling Skills for Professional Persuaders
   Powerful Persuasion Techniques for the 90s
   Establishing Instant Rapport
   Overcoming Hidden Objections
   Surefire Closing Techniques
   How to Get an Endless Supply of Referrals
Available: In person or by videocassette

Contact:

Jack Davis and Associates
25108 Marguerite Parkway, Suite B-209
Mission Viejo, CA 92692

1-800-336-3609
714-583-9271 (in California)

Selling Skills for Loan Originators

"There's nothing like the hand of experience."

Jack Davis:

Here's a man whose background spans all levels of the industry. In mortgage lending since 1974, Jack Davis has been everything from an "on the street" loan originator (for four years) to Senior Vice Present Production Manager at a 16-branch mortgage company. Under Davis' training, the sales force of a national mortgage banking company with 55 branches closed $4.5 billion in one year.

Davis instructs the National Mortgage Bankers Association's Sales Techniques for Loan Originators course. He's trained more than 30,000 salespeople in mortgage banking and real estate.

He holds a bachelor's degree from the University of Wisconsin and a master's degree from Michigan State in Education, and was an instructor for three years in the University of Wisconsin system.

There's no substitute for experience. Call Jack Davis & Associates, (800) 336-3609. In California, (714) 583-9271.

Bill Evans—
Sales Techniques for Loan Originators
    Service-Oriented Selling
    Fighting the Price Battle
    Selling Skill Reality Check
    Where is Your Time Spent?
    Developing Your Sales Plan
    Collateral Material Action Plan
    Telephone Skills
    Dissecting a Sales Call A to Z
    Selling Against the Competition
    Maximizing Your Sales Tools
    Defining Your Market
    Presentation Skills
    Specific Selling Skills
    Handling Objections

Available: In person or by audio cassette

Contact:

Institute of Professional Training
4459 S.E. State Highway, Suite 160A
Port Orchard, Washington 98366
Tel. (206) 871-7574, Fax (206) 871-2464

William H. Evans, Jr.

Bill Evans established the Institute of Professional Training in 1979 as a private training and educational consulting firm specializing in developing marketing and management skills for personnel in the mortgage banking and real estate lending fields.

A graduate of the University of Washington, Bill has authored a number of books, one of which is published by the MBA, *Sales Techniques for Loan Originators*. He has had several of his articles published in the *Mortgage Banking Magazine* and *Real Estate Finance Today* on topics such as sales management in a mortgage banking environment, teambuilding, maximizing direct consumer contact, and customer service.

Bill is an innovative speaker who has a clear understanding of the mortgage industry, as well as human nature. He entertains his audience while instructing them, creating a relaxed environment while addressing serious topics. The comments he makes are easily identifiable, directly applicable and pertinent to everyday situations. His programs specifically address increasing production through management development, loan originator and support staff training.

As a member of the MBA, Bill conducts programs throughout the United States. Since 1981, he has worked solely within the real estate financial services industry. He is a frequent speaker for MBA State Association conferences and seminar leader for individual lenders. He is also an instructor for the School of Mortgage Banking.

Jim Pratt & Todd Duncan—
Selling Skills for Mortgage Loan Professionals

Selling Skills:
  The Profile of a Professional
  The Sales Process
  Getting to the Customer
  Avoiding Call Reluctance
  Time/Territory Management
  Success Strategies
  Effective Listening
  Relationship Building
  Client Seminars

Understanding The Customer:
  Interpersonal Relationships
  Self/Professional Analysis
  Image Management
  The Social Styles
  Discovering Styles
  Managing Styles
  Approaching Styles
  High Performance Prospecting
  Value Added Service

Becoming Your Own Manager:
  Attitude Management
  Cementing Relationships
  Stress Management
  Performance Evaluation
  Mind Management
  Telephone Techniques
  Effective Public Speaking
  Profitable Goal Setting

Available in person or in book form.

Contact:

The Pratt·Duncan Group
8380 Miramar Mall, Suite 225
San Diego, California 92121
619-457-1244

Resident of La Jolla, California

Jim Pratt and Todd Duncan

Responding to the demand to learn his successful methods, Jim has presented seminars and workshops both nationally and internationally. The basis of his successful concepts was learned, tested and proven in the cauldron of the marketplace. He studies theory, but speaks from actual experience, supported with a constant search for the most productive path. Jim is a consummate professional.

Todd's professional speaking and training career has evolved from 9 years of experience in virtually all facets of loan production. As a mortgage lender, Todd has successfully trained hundreds of loan officers and branch managers in successful selling, sales managment, and leadership skills increasing their success dramatically. Specializing in the industry Todd grew up in, he combines his hard earned street degree with his unique ability to train, creating improved results in production and leadership performance. Today, Todd speaks to more than 5,000 loan officers and managers each year, teaching them the skills for peak performance.

The Pratt-Duncan Group is both a training firm and a speakers bureau specializing in improved productivity through people development. The Pratt-Duncan Group seeks the opportunity to explore with you ways to assist you in your search for improvement and to provide professional speakers demonstrably qualified to meet your needs.

Debra Jones—
The Blending Worlds of Sales and Mortgage Banking

Targeting Your Marketplace: Originators running their business like a business rather than operating from a generalized point of view.

Bringing the Business In: Creating marketing ideals developed that will insure a competitive edge. Be assured of getting in to see who they need to see, when they need to see them. Their potential client will be eager to hear what they have to say.

Keeping It: Follow-through once the business has been brought to them. Various approaches to procedurally ensure their clients will receive outstanding service instead of lip service. Domino one transaction into 3 to 5 more.

Available: In person, audiocassette, videocassette (specifically on telephone sales), *Mortgage Generator Newsletter.*

Contact:

Hark and Associates
P. O. Box 2177
Carefree, Arizona 85377-2177
602-678-4071
Order Center: 1-800-456-1001

Appendix

Developing a Marketing Plan

Our marketing plan will actually be a summary of the information presented in this book: An outline that will take us through the steps necessary to prepare and implement a plan to become a producing loan originator. All facets of this model plan are not possible in the real world and you can inject other facets. Yet the basic design, organization, and content can become a blueprint for someone just starting, moving into a new territory, or attempting to reorganize, redirecting or expanding their marketing efforts.

Originator Marketing Plan

Tools of the Trade

- Calculator
- Pager (numeric display)
- Telephone answering machine or service
- Voice mail box or pager
- Car phone

- Personal computer with word processing and publishing software
- Business card

Education

- Real estate license preparation course
- Product knowledge
    1. FHA, VA, State Bond Issue Programs: downpayment, eligibility, and costs
    2. Conventional: conforming and jumbo
       Loan Types: adjustables, growing equity, buydowns, investor
    3. Company's specific products and lock options
- Qualification
    1. Income stability and variability
    2. Credit
    3. Cash
    4. Property
    5. Prequalifications
- Mortgage Processes
    1. Taking an application
    2. Processing
    3. Underwriting
    4. Settlements
- Field Work
    1. Sitting in on applications
    2. Sitting in on prequalifications
    3. Sitting in on rate calls
    4. Sitting in on sales meetings

5. Sitting in on seminars

6. Going out with experienced originator on cold calls

7. Going out with experienced originator on office visits

8. Going out with experienced originator on builder visits

Marketing Preparation

- Develop application packages and extra forms file
- Organize program highlights or product guidelines
- Develop introductory letter and/or package
- Develop and organize marketing materials into marketing books:
    1. Prequalification materials
    2. Referral letters
    3. Flyers on all products and services
    4. Product comparisons and open house spread sheets
- Develop mailing list and referral network
    1. Friends
    2. Co-workers and mortgage industry contacts (include banks, savings and loans, and credit unions).
    3. Real estate agents
    4. Top producers
    5. New agents
    6. Sales managers
    7. Organizations (personal membership)
    8. Financial planners
    9. Settlement agents
    10. Builders
- Organize territory
    1. Key offices

    2.   Key agents

    3.   Peripheral offices

    4.   Subdivisions

Initial marketing

- Initial visits to offices; introduce to receptionist/office manager
- Initial calls for referrals to contact list
- Initial calls for referrals to contact list
- Follow-up mailing with calls to key agents and managers to set up appointments

Marketing plan

- Visit key offices three times per week
  1. Rate sheet before weekend
  2. Newsletter every two weeks (before sales meeting)
  3. Status sheet every Friday
  4. Program flyers to fill in after 1-3
- Visit subdivisions once a week
- Visit peripheral offices once every two weeks
  1. Mail newsletter in off week
  2. Alternate rate sheet and program flyer
- Prepare two open house spread sheets each week: visit Sundays
- Mailing List
  1. Complete list every two weeks, newsletter or program types
  2. Individual letters to key players: five a day
  3. Specialized mailings to categories: one time each month for each category (one per week)
     a. Agents, sales managers, and builders
     b. Settlement agents

    c.   Financial planners

    d.   Friends, former applicants, and refi-candidates

4.   Individual letters to new acquaintances the same day of meeting:

    a.   New agents

    b.   Individuals

    c.   Fellow mortgage bankers

- Meetings

  1.   One sales meeting each week (scheduled or not)

  2.   One seminar every other week (group or individual)

  3.   One lunch each week with key agent or sales manager

  4.   One appointment with Realtor, sales manager, builder, settlement agent, or financial planner each day or if no appointment

- Telephone Calls

  1.   Five calls to key agents each day (mailing follow up)

  2.   One cold call to referral each day

  3.   Three calls to mailing list target each day